The Valley of the Shadow of DEATH

*A mother's journey
through the dark days of grief…
to a brighter tomorrow.*

Judy A. Andres

ISBN 978-0-7414-3455-5

Cover designed by Judy A. Andres

Edited by Ruth A. Bahr

Published by:

INFINITY
PUBLISHING.COM

1094 New DeHaven Street, Suite 100
West Conshohocken, PA 19428-2713
Info@buybooksontheweb.com
www.buybooksontheweb.com
Toll-free (877) BUY BOOK
Local Phone (610) 941-9999
Fax (610) 941-9959

Printed in the United States of America

Published September 2006

FOREWORD

During the past 15 years since my daughter's death, I have written in countless journals, and have written many poems to help me work through the intense feelings I was struggling with. As I have shared them with friends, they have encouraged me to put them together in a book, setting forth the story of my experience, dealing with the death of my child, and why the poems came into being.

I have written this book with the hope that it will help others who are faced with life after the death of their child. If the Lord uses it to help even one person, I will feel as though my efforts have not been in vain.

Judy A. Andres

Photo taken by Nelson's Photography
of Richland Center, WI

(After Jenni died, Jim Nelson graciously gave me all the negatives to the photos he had taken of her.)

This book is dedicated to my Lord and Savior, Jesus Christ, without whom I could have never made the journey. And also to my husband, John, and my son, Dan, who both graciously sacrificed their own privacy so that others might be helped. And last, but not least, to my best friend, Ruth (Lytle) Bahr, who spent countless hours assisting me with the editing of this book.

CONTENTS

POEMS FROM MY HEART

GRADUATION 1991

NEW YORK TRIP

PUPPIES

The Valley of the Shadow of Death

*A mother's journey
through the dark days of grief...
to a brighter tomorrow.*

CHAPTER ONE

*"Even though I walk through the valley of the shadow of death, I will fear
no evil, for you are with me; your rod and your staff, they comfort me."*

Psalm 23:4

In life we are all well aware that there are no guarantees. The natural order of things, or so it has seemed for the majority of my life, is that we are born, we grow up, we grow old, and ultimately we die...preferably of old age, of course. We don't really like it, but the cold, hard truth of the matter is that we all die. No one lives forever. There is no getting around it.

The old saying is very true...the only sure things in life are death and taxes. Unfortunately, we know when taxes are due every year, but maybe fortunately, we can't be that sure of when we are going to die. We just know that we will. We accept it as being part of life. But, it is always so much harder to accept when the person who dies hasn't reached that "magic ripe old age."

When we are young, old can mean anyone over the age of 20. But as the years go by, and we ourselves attain whatever age it was that we considered to be old, that age gradually gets years and years added to it. Before long, a person needs to be at least in their 90's, or maybe even 100 years old, for us to consider them old. Funny how our perspective changes over time as to what age "old" really is.

I'm going to start telling you about my journey by beginning when I was seven years old. At that time I also had a younger sister, Joanne Marie Chapman (now

Sundsmo), who was five. We experienced our first real "tragedy" when our mom, Gertrude Bertha Chapman (Skolaski) died from that dreadful "c" word…cancer.

At the time of her death she was thirty, which, at that time of my life didn't really seem all that young to me. That is, not until my perspective on age changed the closer I got to age thirty. I remember thinking, "Man, this is how old Mom was when her life here on earth was over." And then it hit me, thirty really was not that old. It was, in fact, quite a young age at which to die, especially when she died leaving behind a loving husband and two young children. I remember wondering what she must have felt like, knowing her life was about over. Being excited to go to meet her loving Savior, yet wanting to be here as my sister and I grew up.

I remember praying and asking God that when I had children, He would grant me the privilege of at least seeing them grow to adulthood before He called me home.

In anticipation of leaving my sister and me, Mom wrote a letter to me when she was very ill, and she had our grandmother hand-write a copy for my younger sister. It was to be given to us at a more suitable age, when we would better understand it, and all that had gone on. (It can be found in Appendix A.)

Although it was devastating to have our mom sick, we really believed that she would get well. After all, we were all praying that God would heal her. When He didn't, I thought my world had come to an end. There were some very traumatic years following her death. As I grew older, though, it still seemed within the realm of the natural order of life. A parent had given birth to a child. She had gotten older and sick; she had died. Then the child had to bury the parent and mourn the loss of one of the family matriarchs, as well as the loss of the future with that parent. Even though my dad remarried several years later, providing a wonderful mother, Vivian Mae Martin, and we were blessed with five more siblings, Rebecca Sue Chapman, Philip Arden Chapman, Steven Martin Chapman, Sonya Jean

Chapman (now Schultz) and Ronda Jane Chapman (now Kopfhamer), there were still times, my wedding day, or when my two children were born, that I longed for my mother to be there with me. But, as traumatic as that was for all concerned, we all lived through it and our faith in God grew stronger because of it.

God has promised in His word that He will not give us more than we can bear. Sometimes as we are going through trials in our life we wonder if He really has a handle on just how much we can actually bear. It seems to us, in the midst of the trial, that there is no way we will be able to handle it. That is true, we can't. But God has promised to be there, and to help us, and He is faithful to that promise.

I do, however, remember always being afraid that something was going to happen to my dad or my sister almost any time I wasn't with them. That fear came partially because Mom's headstone had Dad's name on it, too. I remember thinking that meant my dad must be sick and going to die, just like Mom had. I don't remember ever asking him about it, but I worried that was what it meant. I would worry about what I would do if that did happen. I even prayed that if one of us had to die, that it would be me. Silly me, as if I could make a deal with God and seal the safety of the rest of my family. I must admit, I had a selfish motive in praying like that. I didn't want to have to go on living through losing anyone else I loved.

Because of losing a parent to death, I had traveled down the dark shadowy road of grief, even though at the time I didn't understand that was what I was feeling and having to deal with. I just knew that nothing worse had ever happened to me, and I didn't want it to ever happen again.

I felt abandoned. I felt like I wanted to die, and I longed to be able to go to be with Mom. I felt physically ill, and very scared and unsure for a long time. I remember crying uncontrollably from time to time for years afterward.

I knew what it was like to lose someone I loved very dearly. So, as I grew to adulthood and had two children of my own, I remember praying and almost begging God to keep them safe, and not to let anything happen to take them from me. I had even voiced that by saying, "I don't think I could go on living if something were to happen to either of my children." I'm quite sure that anyone who is a parent feels the same way. Our children are a gift from God, and there is nothing we wouldn't do for them to keep them safe and happy.

I have been given what most people might think is the perfect American family - a mom, a dad, and two children...a girl and a boy. If I could have had my way, I would have had a dozen kids, but unfortunately my husband was not of the same persuasion. Being perfectly honest, I probably would have settled for six. However, my husband's compromise was to have two, and two were far better than none. The only change I would have made with the two kids we have would have been to have the boy first, and then the girl. I was the oldest of seven in the Arden Chapman family, and always wished I'd had a big brother to look out for me. But, God didn't see it the same way I did, which really should come as no surprise. We often differ on the perfect outcome of my prayers. Our daughter was born first, and then our son, three-and-a-half years later. I find it rather funny in this day and age that a person can find out ahead of time whether they are having a boy or a girl, but only God determines the sex. Once our two children were born, God must have determined that our quiver was full. (Lo, children are an heritage of the Lord: and the fruit of the womb is his reward. As arrows are in the hand of a mighty man; so are children of the youth. Happy is the man that hath his quiver full of them...Ps. 127:3-5a)

CHAPTER TWO

"The Lord giveth and the Lord taketh away, blessed be the name of the Lord."

Job 2:21b

My husband, John Arthur Andres, and I were married December 18, 1971. I thank God for the wonderful husband he gave me. One that loves me regardless of the rough times we have gone through. He always has said, "When I said, "I do", I did." I have come to realize over the years, just how lucky I am to have him in my life.

God graciously gave John and me two beautiful children. Our daughter, Jennifer Lyn Andres, was born Tuesday, May 29, 1973, at 10:50 A.M. Our son, Daniel John Andres, followed 3½ years later, sneaking in on Tuesday, October 26, 1976, just three minutes past midnight. They are the pride of my life.

From the start, Jenni seemed to rush life. Looking back I often wonder if God had given her some inner knowledge that time was short, and she needed to make the most of every minute of the day and night. From birth on she slept very little, and when she did, it was a restless sleep. She was walking by the time she was barely 8 months old. I remember one time when she was in the hospital for pneumonia, and had gotten to feeling better, we were walking the halls and some of the nurses said I shouldn't be making her walk so young. I asked them just exactly how I was supposed to make her not walk. She'd already been doing it since she was just barely 8 months old. I wasn't "making" her walk. She also talked in sentences when she was 1½ years old. She learned to ride her two-wheeler when she was still four.

People always commented on how well she'd carry on conversations with adults, when she was only a few

5

years old. I attributed that to the fact that I wanted someone to talk to, being a stay-at-home mom, and so I probably talked to her a lot. I didn't really want her talking baby talk, so I'd talk to her as if she were an adult. It must have rubbed off.

I always thought she tried to grow up way too fast. But, you know moms; we'd like to keep our kids little as long as we can.

Jenni was very outgoing as a youngster. She would go to anyone, which always made me a little nervous. You never want your children to be afraid of everyone, but you'd like them to have a little bit of healthy fear of strangers.

As much as she enjoyed being an athlete, she wasn't nearly as naturally athletic as her brother, Dan, and that irritated her some. I think it was because she was somewhat of a perfectionist, and if she couldn't do it perfectly, she didn't like doing it. She never liked it when Dan could do something better than she could. I remember when we got our first boat and the kids were learning to water ski. She and Dan both learned fast, but Dan, by far, was the better skier, and he was 3½ years younger than Jenni. I could tell it bothered her when he wanted to learn to slalom (ski on one ski) and he did it with little trouble. Even though she really had no desire to ski like that, she tried and tried until she could finally ski on one ski, too. She wasn't going to let her little brother one up her.

She was also what you might call rather klutzy. She had the unusual habit of falling on the stairs. Not "down" the stairs, like you might think most people do. Rather, she would fall "up" the stairs.

Jenni was always worried about her weight. I remember how bad she felt when she reached the age where she weighed 100 pounds. You'd have thought that she had just been told that the world was coming to an end. "I can't weigh that much!" she shrieked. I tried to comfort her, and assure her that 100 pounds was not much for her to weigh, considering how tall she was, and that it would be very unhealthy if she weighed any less than that at her age and height. I even used the, "Your bone structure is heavier than mine, and so you are always going to weigh more than 100 pounds. Your bones probably weigh that much." My reassurances didn't help much to ease her troubled mind. She continued to worry about her weight pretty much the rest of her life. I recall one time when she was heading over to the college campus gym to do aerobics and exercise more because she had eaten a Snickers bar earlier that day, and she didn't want to gain weight from it. That was one of the few sweet things she liked. She wasn't much for eating things like that. (Got to watch the weight you know.)

She was a great one for writing letters that she never mailed. I'd find them all over the house. I'd say, "Jen, do you want me to mail this letter for you?" She'd usually say, "No thanks, Mom. I wrote it a few days/weeks ago, and the news is old." I'd say, "Not to the person you wrote the letter to, if you never mailed it. Why don't you let me send it anyway. I'm sure they'd like to hear from you." And she'd say, "No, throw it out. I'll write a new one." I found several of just such letters in her room after she died, and I mailed some of them anyway.

Jenni often turned on lights all over the house. She didn't like the dark. In July of 1991, John, Dan and I had gone with the local church youth group to Colorado for a week on a camping trip to hike Mt. Harvard, one of the Fourteeners in the Collegiate Mountain Range. (By the way, "fourteener" refers to elevation, and the fact that the mountain is 14,000 feet or more above sea level.) Jenni had stayed home by herself because she had a job and had already taken off to go to New York. If the truth were told, she really had no desire anyway to hike a mountain. Although she liked camping, she wasn't into camping where there were no bathrooms. Now that I think about it, I suppose that might have been why none of the girls in the youth group at church had gone either. When we got back, in the middle of the day, every single light inside the house was on, from the basement to the bedrooms upstairs, as well as the outside yard light, and she wasn't even home. She was at work. She was great about turning the lights on, but it was a constant battle to get her to turn them off. A neighbor later told me it had been pretty bright at our house while we were gone.

Something else she was great at, from the time she was about 1 year old, was changing clothes. She always wanted to dress herself. She would be off playing so well, but so quietly, and I'd be just about ready to go see what she was into, when she'd come out wearing something entirely different than what I had dressed her in that morning. I have a photo of her one day when she decided that she wanted to go outside. It was winter at the time. She had taken off all her clothes and put her blue corduroy winter coat on backwards, with her red mittens on her feet. The mittens were the kind that had the string connecting them together. What a sight! She was pretty proud of herself. I still smile when I think about it.

That never changed. Not even when she got to be a teenager. In fact, it was worse. She'd go through several outfits a day. I used to get a little perturbed at her when I'd do the laundry because I'd find clothes in the dirty clothes that I knew I had just washed, but not seen her wear. Upon doing a little investigative work on my own, super sleuth that I am, I discovered that most of the time it was because she had tried them on and decided not to wear them, and then tossed them off to the side, trying something else on until she'd find what she wanted to wear. Then she'd put them all in the dirty clothes because they were wrinkled. I finally put my foot down. "Jen," I told her, "you've got to knock this off. I refuse to wash clean clothes. If you can't hang them up after you're done trying them on, then you're going to have to start doing your own laundry." That helped for a brief time, but never really did solve the problem completely.

I used to find the drawers of my dresser left open after she had made a whirlwind trip through my room to grab some item of my clothing that she thought she so desperately needed to complete her ensemble for the day. That's what happens when you and your daughter wear the same size. I never really minded that she'd borrow things, I just would have preferred that she at least shut the drawers.

I was looking through some of the things I had saved over the years, and I came across an assignment Jenni had completed for Independent Living Class her senior year. She wrote it March 18, 1991. It was her "Autobiography," and the following are some excerpts from it, which may give you a little insight into who she was, from her own words. They must have been given a list of questions or topics that were to be included in their autobiography. The first section was entitled "ROOTS," in which she gave the general history of when and where she was born, and all the places we had lived. I personally liked the part in that section about our vacations:

> Some of the most special times in my life have been on vacation. I had a lot of fun on our family vacations. Over the years my family and I have went (sic) to a lot of places. I loved our Florida vacations, and our New York trip was a lot of fun too. I loved the summer we went to Maine. I will never forget sitting on the beach watching the sun come up and getting eaten alive by hungry Maine mosquitoes. I also had a great time in Lake Placid watching the U.S. Freestyle Ski Team practicing, and climbing to the top of the Statue of Liberty in record time was a blast too. My parents have given me a lot of opportunities to see a lot of things, and all of them are very special to me. I remember one time when we were in Washington. All of us thought it would be fun to go deep sea fishing. I was so sick. I will just say that I will never ever do that again for any reason. It was definitely memorable.

The next section of the autobiography was entitled "JOBS."

In the future I hope to either work as a translator, or do something in the psychology field. Both of these fields interest me very much. I haven't decided which one to major in yet.

The best job that I could imagine is kind of a tough question, because I have very little knowledge about jobs and what they entail. I would imagine that it would be something like having my own schedule for being a translator, and to translate in really exotic places. Or maybe, it would mean that I would have a high position in a psychology lab, and be able to research the things that interest me the most. No matter what I do, I think that the best possible job I could imagine would be one that would be challenging, but fulfilling. I want to be happy far more than I want to be filthy rich, but if the two came together, I can't see myself complaining one bit.

Then came "PERSONALITY."

I am a little bit afraid of doing this section because I do not want to sound like I'm conceited, but I don't want to sell myself short either. I guess I have good listening skills, because a lot of people will come to me to talk. I like to think that I am a good friend too, because I have great friends, and I have had them for quite a long time. I have interests in foreign culture, and psychology as I mentioned before, and I love music.

I have some nervous habits, like biting my fingernails occasionally, and drumming my fingers. This is not that outstanding or anything, it is just something that I always do. I used to have a habit of procrastination, but I am a lot better than I used to be.

I like things to go smoothly, but I hate having to stick to the same old schedules all the time. I like a little spontaneity in life. Like I said before, I love music, as well as art and literature. I think that a classical education is good in conjunction with new, fun twists that make things more true to life. I appreciate this class, I even like it, even though it isn't always very fun. (This is supposed to be humorous.)

As far as inner feelings go, that is kind of private don't you think. Since this is a report though, I will let you in on some of the basics. I trust completely, but not easily. I am afraid of getting burned again. I am very protective of my friends, and I would do anything for the close ones. I am close to my family on the whole, although we have our moments that aren't too close. I don't think this is unusual though. I promote the idea of living in peace, but I realize that sometimes war is necessary. I like to try new things, but sometimes I am hesitant, I don't always prefer to jump in blindly, so to speak.

"SPARE TIME" was the next category:

I think favorite places are hard to name because I have a lot of them. One of my favorite places is up north. I worked at a camp for two summers, and it is one of my favorite places because of the people and the things that we did there. Another favorite place is my grandparents' cottage on a lake. It reminds me of the way things used to be when I was little, a lot has changed since then, and it is nice to remember when everything was happy and uncomplicated. Upstate New York is another of my favorite places. I have friends who live in the mountains, and one of the places they took me to is really special to me.

I spend money on vacations and trips. For a long time I saved to go to Europe, and I didn't spend a whole lot of money on anything else. Now I am saving my money for a trip to New York this summer with Jennifer. We will be taking a train and we will be gone for two weeks, so I am trying not to spend a whole lot of money until then.

I could tell you a lot more meaningless stuff about myself, but I think that I have fulfilled the requirements, and I am sure that you have a lot of these to grade. So, enough is enough, and when do we get to know some of these same things about you? I hope this isn't too tough of a question.

Her teacher replied:

That's not a tough question – we'll have to talk together sometime. I enjoyed reading your autobiography. Save this to read again in the future – you are a special person that I've appreciated having in class.

Her teacher gave her 100/100, and Jenni was very happy with that grade. Jenni was always pretty hard on herself when it came to her grades. Anything less than 100 percent usually upset her. I suppose that's the perfectionist in her again. But just so you know, Jenni was not a whiz kid. She studied hard for her grades.

There was one particular speech outline that made me smile. I thought I'd share it with you, too, since it also lets you in on who she was. It was entitled, "Backseat Drivers." The introduction went like this:

I.   I think I can safely assume that each of us has had at least some contact with backseat drivers. In fact, many of us have been backseat drivers at some point in our lives. I don't know why this is, I don't understand it...it just happens. Maybe it's hereditary, because everyone in my family is a backseat driver. We each have our own way of approaching it, but there's no doubt that we're all guilty.

II.   I'll begin with myself. (*Teacher comment: Good way to begin*)

12

1. Occasional – tendency surfaces when dad drives.
2. Annoyed by 5 m.p.h. under the speed limit
3. "Dad, its okay to go the speed limit."
4. Embarrassing to go 60 on the Interstate.

III. My Father.

   1. The habitual backseat driver–hereditary?
   2. Disapproving grunts and noises, drumming fingers. *(Teacher comment: Nice details)*
   3. Picky – "signal sooner, slow more gradual."
   4. Things that bother no one but him.

IV. My Mother.

   1. The more subtle type *(Teacher comment: Nice difference)*
   2. Politely comments, "Jen, it might be a good idea to slow down just a bit, don't you think?"
   3. Disguises her tension and nervousness.
   4. Kind you don't really mind.

V. My Brother. *(Teacher comment: You saved the best for last!)*

   1. The rude backseat driver.
   2. Kind you'd love to strangle after they scream.
   3. "STOP!" in the middle of a block. *(Teacher comment: Funny)*
   4. "COPS!" as you're cruising on the Interstate.

VI.   Conclusion.

So, the next time you find yourself correcting the way someone else is driving, remember how you felt about the last backseat driver who rode with you; you may wish to bite your tongue. *(Teacher comment: Excellent advice)*

Her teacher gave Jen a 10/10 on her outline, and 18/20 on her speech, and wrote:

Fine speech. Nice command of the language – well-organized details – Good delivery – Looked happy and calm (even if you didn't feel calm) – We will! (referring to biting the tongue.)

Jenni had a wide variety of topics that she wrote essays and speeches on. Here are some of the others: A Burning Issue: Flag Desecration, The Mystery of ESP, Feedback, and Child Abuse, just to name a few.

She also wrote the following poems. I wonder if that is hereditary. My mom wrote poetry (her poetry is in Appendix A), I obviously have dabbled in it, and Jen did, too. Some were untitled, as is this first one I'm sharing with you:

UNTITLED

By Jennifer Lyn Andres

A rainbow may mean many things,
To some new hope it seems to bring.
The hope that will renew the zeal
That once gave life a good appeal.
Now you stand upon your own.
You wonder what you've really done.
Your life is blowing in the wind.
Leaves you wondering where you've really been.

Your life is seeming less like the rainbow,
More like the storm.
You've now realized every rose has its thorn.
You wish upon a dream you once knew.
You're wondering if they do come true.
Then something takes you by surprise.
There's more than darkness in your skies.
I can only wonder if you knew,
Just who really believed in you.

IMAGINARY FRIENDS

By Jennifer Lyn Andres

Before I fall asleep at night
I think about my dreams.
I wish there really was a place
Where things were as they seem.
I think about reality
And how painful it can be.
How I wish you only were
Here again with me.
A lot has changed for everyone
Since you're not around.
Now all of my best memories
Have been put in the ground.
I think of you when I'm alone.
I cry since you're not here.
Though I know it does no good,
My tears will never bring you back,
But how I wish they could.
Things would be much safer if
People lived in dreams.
There would be no imaginary friends,
No lies, no silent screams.
I know there is a time when
Every dream will end.
But in reality
I'm living in a world of
Imaginary friends.

FOREVER FRIENDS

By Jennifer Lyn Andres

Forever friends have lots to share.
Forever friends try not to have an unhappy glare.
They try not to get mad,
even if things start off bad.
Forever friends always have time to give.
Forever friends make a better life to live.
They try not to leave when things go wrong.
Instead, they're there with a song.
Even if they cannot be there when you need them,
You known they really tried, and
Forever friends have forever friendship so
It makes it feel like they're at your side.
Forever friendship should be treasured
Because not all friendships last forever.
If you need this kind of friend ask someone
And if you're lucky they'll stay
with you to the end.
Forever friends will never part
Because their friendship comes from the heart.

THE BROKEN HEART

By Jennifer Lyn Andres

You will, I'm sure, find my friend, the heart is fragile, it has only one way to end. It often cries, but is not heard, for the crying heart speaks not a word. It cries in time when sorrow comes, and it splits apart in pain. Yet still its cry is heard by one, and often unsuccessfully shoved away in pain, only to return crying without seeming end. When this takes place, at least in me, I find when the heart gets so suddenly and silently torn apart, and while it's crying without seeming end, the pain doth yet increase again. This might happen only once or twice I hope in any given person's life. It seems as when the heart truly cries, that a part of it does often die, and part of you is left in pain, for there is that much less of you to learn to feel again. So cry on for now my aching heart, but do try not to let it get the best part. You easily tell what that part is, for where it hurts you the most is where it is. Like I said before, cry my heart that's broke in two. Sometimes they say it can be good for you. Someday, my friend, this lonely, painful, sad time will surely end. But until then, try to get through. Just remember, all the others who feel just as bad as you.

CHAPTER THREE

"...As is the mother, so is her daughter."

Ezekiel 16:44b

Our son, Dan, had saved his snow shoveling money and in the summer of 1991, had bought an airline ticket to go visit his Uncle Todd, who was stationed in Hawaii. Dan was 14 at the time, and I hated to see him go all that way alone, but figured it would be good for him to be a little more independent. We were all sitting at the airport, waiting for the time of his departure, when Jenni went over and sat along side him. Smiling and taking his hand, she turned towards me and said, "Quick, Mom, take a picture of Dan and me getting along, in case something happens to one of us this summer." At the time I figured she was just trying to be funny, and poke fun at what I always told them while they were arguing.

She, herself, was going to be leaving on a trip with a girlfriend to New York a week or so later. We all laughed, and Dan even smiled. Little did I know how precious that photo would be to me.

I remember how apprehensive I was a year earlier when she had taken a trip to France by herself when she was 17, between her junior and senior year of high school. She kept the letter I wrote to her on August 3, 1990, which was one day after she had left France, and I had already talked to her twice. In that letter I was telling her how much I loved her and that I didn't mean to be overprotective...it's just that I loved her so much. I had also put a P.S. on the letter:

> P.S. I saw Karen Fowell today. Had to get her signature on something, and she works at the hospital doing...I'm not sure what. Anyway, I

19

said hello from you, and introduced myself as your mom. She told me she thinks you're a pretty special young lady – and so do I! She says she hopes she has a daughter that turns out just like you. She said she'd be very proud. I told her I'm sure she would, because I am!

Sometimes children tend to think we don't trust them, or we don't want them out of our sight. They think we are half crazy for worrying about them when they are out with friends, or when they get their driver's license and start driving cars. I guess they can't really understand what we go through until they are grown and have children of their own.

I remember all too well the hard time I was having with the fact that my children were growing up, and soon would be leaving. We raise our children to be independent, and we want to make sure we have equipped them with all the skills they will need to be on their own, but when the time approaches for them to fly the nest, it is hard. At least it was for me. I think moms generally have a harder time with it than dads. Sometimes it seemed to me like dads almost looked forward to it going back to being just two again. Of course, I am only speaking from my experience as a mom. John, as the dad, might beg to differ with me.

I'll never forget one of the first times I remember feeling really devastated by what I felt was rejection. Jenni and I had always been very close. I considered her one of my best friends. We did most things together, and talked pretty openly about most anything. Well, after we had moved to Richland Center, I had started taking a few classes out at the UW Campus. At that time Jenni was just starting in high school, and a new school mind you. We only lived about four or five blocks from the high school and she always walked home.

This particular fall day was a beautiful sunny day. You know the kind. It always warms back up once school starts, making it hard for the kids to get back in the swing of things. They'd rather be outside in the sunny warm weather than sitting inside the stuffy school building. Anyway, I had walked to the campus, rather than drive the mile or so, and was coming home at the same time she would be getting out of school and be walking home. I figured I'd just swing by the school and walk home with her, so she didn't have to walk by herself. Boy was that a mistake! Bad move on my part. When I called to get her attention, and she turned around and saw it was me, she frantically signaled for me to back off, and she crossed over and walked on the other side of the street. I was crushed. I imagine she just didn't want to be seen at the new school with her mommy walking her home. Wouldn't do much for a gal's image, or make a very good first impression.

When it came time for the kids to get their driver's licenses, I was the one who taught them to drive. Their dad really didn't have the patience for it, and I didn't mind. They didn't seem as nervous with me anyway. Jenni was pretty proud when she learned to drive a standard transmission. So much so that she even decided to teach a friend who had never driven one. She took our little pickup truck and went to an empty parking lot so she could help her friend learn to drive a stick. She thrived on being the one who was in charge, which usually caused tension between her and her brother, for obvious reasons.

As Jenni and Dan were on their way, growing to adulthood, I remember wondering what life was going to be like when they were gone from home, and dreaded the day it would become a reality. When they were young, my time was consumed with raising them and caring for their every need. As they grew and became more and more independent, I found myself feeling less and less needed, at least in my own mind, and I didn't like that feeling. I think Jenni felt the vibes, because one day out of the blue she said to me, "Mom, you really need to get a life. Dan and I aren't going to be here forever."

Jenni had grown into a beautiful young woman. Blonde hair, blue eyes, and fair skin. She had a very fiery disposition, and talked almost nonstop. I used to ask her, as she'd follow me around the house talking from one subject to another, and then another, almost without taking a breath, if she had something against peace and quiet. We'd both laugh, and then she'd pick up right where she left off, and keep right on talking. One time she wrote me a 7-page letter from Bible camp, and ended it by writing: "I figured if I write a lot each week, when I get home I won't talk you to death." I couldn't help but laugh, and I thought, "Yeh, right! Like that will make any difference!"

She also had a way of driving me to the brink of tears, by always wanting the last word, and never knowing when it was time to back off and leave well enough alone. I think she would have made a good lawyer. She seemed to love a good debate, and rarely ever backed down. It got her into trouble with her dad on more than one occasion.

She and her brother could get into some pretty nasty squabbles at times, too. I would tell them they were acting like 2-year-olds, and say they shouldn't talk like that to each other, because if something were to happen to one of them, they'd feel really bad about all the fighting they did.

CHAPTER FOUR

"...behold, now is the accepted time; now is the day of salvation."

II Corinthians 6:2b

Jenni was 18, and planning on going to college after she graduated (in 1991). She talked about going for a degree in psychology, or maybe becoming something like a social worker, or some similar line of work. In the process of trying to figure out where she wanted to go to college, I had managed to talk her into staying in Richland Center where we lived, and attending the UW Extension Campus, thereby being able to live at home. I told her that it was because the classes that she would take the first couple years would be the same basic courses as she would take anywhere else. Those classes were offered at the Richland Campus, and it would be so much cheaper. If I were to be completely honest, it was probably so that I wouldn't have to let go of her as soon. In my mind, she would be so much safer at home.

During the summer, she had started dating Kevin Knause. He had recently gotten out of the Marines, and had planned to attend the UW campus at Richland Center. I think she had told me he had been a friend of her former boyfriend. I honestly can't remember how she said they met. Kevin was nearly five years her senior. We only met him a couple times, so we really did not know him very well. He was rather quiet, at least around us, and I remember thinking that maybe that was good, because Jenni did like to talk.

She started classes at the Richland Campus in September. She was very busy, between working at a local grocery store, going to classes every weekday, doing the homework, and spending time with her new boyfriend, Kevin.

Unfortunately, my keeping her at "home" hadn't really done what I thought it might – give me a little more time with her. She was getting up early and coming home late every day. I rarely saw her.

I was feeling pretty dejected and sorry for myself when, on Wednesday, October 2, 1991, she called me at work to ask, "Mom, do you have time to go to lunch with me?" I have to admit I got a little miffed at her asking me if I had time. After all, I reasoned, it wasn't me who was never around. So, I said, "Me have time? I'm not the one who doesn't have time for you." She just laughed at me, and repeated her invitation, which I gladly accepted.

She came by the law office where I worked to get me, and we headed to Pizza Hut. Who doesn't like pizza! As we headed out to the car, she asked if I wanted to drive. She said, "I know my driving makes you nervous," (even though she felt she was an excellent driver) and she smiled at me. I told her, "No, that's okay. Go ahead and drive. I trust you."

Over lunch, we talked, or rather she talked, like usual. I listened, smiling over how some things never change. I taught her to talk early, and she had never stopped once she started. That day was no different. She talked about a lot of things, but one thing sticks out in my mind. She said, "Mom, last night Kevin and I really talked. We spent the whole night talking about what we believed. What we believed about who Jesus is, and what He means to me, and things like that." She said, "We talked for hours." Then she asked, "Why do you think that was what we talked about, when we've never talked about it before?" I told her I wasn't sure, but maybe God intended her to be a witness to Kevin. As I look back now, I know exactly why that was the topic for the evening. If she asked now, I'd tell her, although I'm sure she knows, that God was giving Kevin one more chance to accept Christ as his Savior, because on Saturday Kevin was going to die.

Then, almost as soon as she had started talking about it, she moved on to another subject, and lunch was over. We left, with her driving, and she dropped me back off at work.

On Friday, October 4th, I had taken off work early so that I could get ready for the company we were expecting that weekend for the Applefest celebration in Richland Center. Our good friends from Crescent Lake Bible Camp, the Bennetts, were coming up from Illinois to spend the weekend with us. I was busy in the kitchen preparing baked goods for our guests. I was on the phone with my friend, Vicki, when I got the call-waiting beep on the phone. Generally, it was my practice not to take a call waiting if I was on a long distance call with someone, but for some reason I did that time. It was Jenni on the other call. I explained to her that I was on the phone with Vicki Bennett, and I asked her what she needed, and if I could just call her back. She hurriedly said, "Nothing important, Mom, I was just checking to see if you were home." And with that, she said good-bye, and I went back to finish my conversation with my friend.

I had not much more than gotten off the phone with Vicki when in Jenni came through the back door. I was surprised to see her because I knew that on Fridays she had classes late, and it was only early afternoon. When I asked her what she was doing home she said, "I always have a 2-hour break between my last two classes, and I thought instead of staying at the campus or going over to Kevin's to work on homework, I'd come home. I miss my mom." I smiled and thought, "Not near as much as I miss you."

She said I didn't have to stop what I was doing; she'd just sit on the step that went upstairs from our kitchen to the kids' bedrooms, and talk to me. Which she did. I kept baking, and she kept talking.

Out of the blue, which she was good at, she asked me if I was disappointed in her. I asked her what she meant by a comment like that. She said she knew lately she had maybe done a couple things that she knew I wasn't that pleased with. She said she knew too that I loved to cook

25

and bake, and she really didn't care to do that much. I reassured her that it didn't disappoint me, and that nothing she could ever do would make me love her any less. I told her not everyone likes the same things as their parents do, so she shouldn't worry about it. I know I told you earlier that I consider her to be a perfectionist, at least when it came to what she expected from herself. I think this demonstrates that quite clearly.

Then she said, "You know how you have always said that if something were to happen to me or Dan that you wouldn't want to go on living?" That brought tears to my eyes, and I didn't really answer her. I just kept doing whatever it was I was doing, in hopes she'd move on to another subject, like she usually did. She just ignored that, and went on, "Well, you know, if I was to die, Dad and Dan would still be here, and they'd still need you." I remember telling her that if she didn't have anything better to talk to me about, maybe she should think about going back to the campus. She changed the subject then, and a little later got up to go upstairs to change her clothes so she could just leave right for work after class.

As she was headed up the stairs, she stopped and came back down and stuck her head around the corner and said, "You know, Mom, lately I've had the strangest feeling that I'm going to see your mom before you do." I told her that would be impossible, as I would die long before she would. At least I figured in the natural order of things that was the way it would be. With that, she smiled and turned and went on upstairs, changed clothes and left without saying much more.

A thought passed through my mind because of her strange conversation. I remembered how several times over the years she had wanted to talk to me about my mom. She'd always ask me how old Mom was when she died, and how she died, and things like that. She'd say how she wished my mom would still be here, and asked if I ever wished that, and on and on. Then she'd say she didn't think

26

she would live as long as that...and she felt that maybe she wouldn't even live to be 20.

I remember her even telling me a couple times that she thought she would die in an accident, and she asked me if I thought that it would hurt. (A friend of the family just told me recently that she remembers hearing Jenni and I talking about that.) I told Jenni I had no way of knowing that, but from the experiences that I had with the accidents that I had been in, I felt it would depend on whether or not you saw it coming, and whether you were to die instantly. Whenever I'd been hurt, I remember the initial pain from the impact, but then it was like I was watching myself in slow motion, and the pain didn't come back until after the accident was all over and the shock and numbness wore off. Then I'd tell her not to be so morbid, and say, "No one knows ahead of time how they are going to die. I suppose, unless they were to take their own life."

I remember hearing her tell me other times that if she was ever in a bad accident that she didn't want me to feel bad or take it wrong, but she wouldn't want to go on living if she wouldn't be 100% okay. She said, "You can call me vain or selfish, or whatever you want, but that is the way I feel." She wouldn't want to live if she'd have to be in a wheelchair or disfigured. I assumed that conversation was sparked because of the teenage boy who lived just down the block from us. He had recently been in a car accident. He was the only one seriously injured. Not really any lasting damage to his physical features, but he was now paralyzed from the waist down, and in a wheelchair for the rest of his life. She seemed to just want me to understand that she didn't think she'd be able to deal with life like that.

CHAPTER FIVE

"For man also knoweth not his time…"

Ecclesiastes 9:12a

I think the hardest thing about October 5th is that I didn't know when Jenni left that afternoon that that would be the last time I saw her. The last time I'd hug her. The last time I'd hear her voice. The last time I'd see her for the rest of my life.

About 11:00 P.M. I was lying awake in bed, waiting for her to get home at whatever time she was going to get home. I always did that any time either one of my kids weren't home. I had to know they were safe at home, or I couldn't go to sleep. It didn't matter what time of night it was.

Then I heard sirens start…first one, and then another, and another. The police went first, followed by the ambulance, and then the fire truck. Siren after siren. I remember looking at the clock and thinking, "It can't be Jenni, it's only 11:00 P.M. and she was going to the late movie in Madison. The movie will barely be over, and at best, she'll just be leaving Madison to head home. It can't be her."

I remember thinking it must be a really bad accident though for all those emergency vehicles to be called out, and I hoped that the people involved weren't anyone that I knew.

I don't doubt that you understand there is no way to prepare for the phone call that comes in the middle of the night when your child is not at home. When the phone started ringing I didn't want to answer it. I let it ring and ring, as my heart started pounding in my ears. I tried to calm my thoughts by reassuring myself that it was way too early for Jenni to be anywhere in the area. Then I thought,

28

"What if it is Jenni, calling to tell me she is going to be later than I think? I better answer it."

I slowly picked up the receiver, cautiously putting it to my ear, all the while praying it was Jenni. But it wasn't her voice that I heard on the other end of the line. It was a male voice. He asked me if I knew where my car was. I don't even remember him telling me who he was, although I'm sure he must have. I told him that our car was probably in Madison. That our daughter had taken it to Madison earlier that day. He asked me how old she was. I told him, "18." He then asked if she would have loaned the car to anyone else. I told him no. He asked me if I was sure. Throughout all his questions I just kept asking him if Jenni was okay. That was really upsetting me. I was asking him if Jenni was okay, and all he was doing was asking me more questions...questions that didn't make any sense to me.

I was getting more and more upset, and by this time my husband was awake and wanting to know what was going on. I held the phone toward him, wanting him to take it and talk, as I was trembling almost uncontrollably, and in tears.

We were told that there had been an accident, but they wouldn't tell us how bad. They asked where we lived, and it just so happened that we only lived a few blocks from the hospital. We rushed there, but they wouldn't let us go in and see her. They said it was because they were working on her, and we might be in the way, or some technique that they had to use might seem rough or cruel, and we wouldn't understand what they were doing as they were trying to get her stabilized.

I knew right away that it was not going to be okay, although those around me kept trying to reassure us that she was strong and she would be okay. Something inside me kept telling me she wouldn't live. Maybe in the back of my mind I felt she wouldn't even try, if she were badly hurt. After all, it had been a head-on collision at highway speed. The emergency crew had to use the Jaws of Life to get Jenni out of the smashed vehicle. There was no way she wouldn't be severely injured.

It is very hard to sit outside an emergency room, waiting, knowing that your child is lying on the other side of the wall, probably dying...or dead. I found it very hard to understand why they wouldn't let me in by her. I had always been there any other time she'd been hospitalized. I felt she needed me by her. Maybe it would help if I were by her, so I could talk to her. Tell her to hang in there. Tell her she was going to be okay.

Eventually I was told that her boyfriend, Kevin, had not made it. In fact, he had been dead at the scene of the accident. Then, around midnight, Mr. Wallace died. He was the man who was driving the car that they had collided with, head-on, at highway speed.

I found out later that not one of them had been wearing their seatbelts. Not that it would have necessarily saved any of them, but it might have. (I found out later that Kevin had just been ticketed a week before for failure to wear his seatbelt.) The rescue crew had been able to open both Kevin and Mr. Wallace's car doors to get them out of the vehicles, so I've always wondered if their lives might not have been spared had they been wearing their seatbelts that night.

Jenni's friends told me they didn't understand why she didn't have her seatbelt on. Just a week or so before, she had put her books on top of the roof of her car and then had driven off with them still on the roof. The books were strewn over a couple block area by the time she realized what she had done. As she went back, driving along, she'd stop by each book, take her seatbelt off and get out of the car and pick the book up. Then she'd get back in the car, put her seatbelt back on, and drive another block or so to the next book. There she'd stop the car and repeat the act until all the books were retrieved. They said she also would not start driving until they put their seatbelts on. So, you can see why it was so hard to accept that she didn't have her seatbelt on that night. I guess only she and God know why she didn't.

That was only part of the mystery and questions that haunted me for a long time. The "how" as well as the "why" of the accident, and not knowing the answers just about drove me crazy. All sorts of thoughts run through a person's head after something happens that they don't have answers for. Did she fall asleep? Did she lean over to wake Kevin up because they were almost home? I found out later from her girlfriend that had gone to Madison with Jenni and Kevin that night, that Kevin hadn't been feeling the greatest. She usually let Kevin drive, but they figure he had his seat reclined and was probably sleeping beside Jenni as she drove home, since he wasn't feeling well. They were almost home...just 4 miles from home to be exact. I measured it several times after the accident. For what reason, I'm not sure.

Rumors fly at times like that. I'm sure, because Jenni was 18 that some might have thought drugs or alcohol were involved, but the police report confirmed that none were. I know anyone who knew Jenni wouldn't have even considered that there had been. Someone even suggested that maybe Kevin had grabbed the steering wheel for some unknown reason. I wondered if the roads were bad because while we were at the hospital that night it started to snow...but at the time of the accident the roads were dry.

Med Flight had been called, but because it had started snowing (October 6th mind you...how often do we get snow in early October?) they had to turn back when they were just five minutes from the Richland Center Hospital where Jenni was waiting to be transported to a Madison hospital. Visibility had gotten bad, and the area they had to land in at the Richland Center Hospital was hard enough to negotiate when they could see well. I often wondered if it would have made any difference, if she would still be alive, had they been able to get to Richland Center and get her to Madison faster.

I wondered, too, if maybe a deer or some other animal might have run out in front of her, causing her to swerve to miss it. But there were people that had followed her for quite a long way, and they hadn't seen anything unusual. They said she had been traveling at the speed limit, and not driving erratically like someone that is in the process of falling asleep would, where they fluctuate in speed or go off onto the shoulder of the road.

I even wondered, for a brief period of time, if she had meant to end her life. I talked to the therapist that she had seen the year before, just to make sure that they had never talked about anything like that. She assured me that the subject had never come up, and that there had been no indication in any of the sessions that Jenni had with her. I had just wondered because of a conversation Jenni had with me the morning of the day that the accident happened. She had been getting ready for work, standing in front of the mirror in my bathroom, and she had started crying. When I asked her what was wrong, she had said, "I'm so tired. Tired of work, tired of school, tired of life." (She was always very dramatic about how she felt.) I got angry with her, and told her she wouldn't be so tired if she'd come home at night and get some sleep. I told her, "If you don't start getting some more sleep, something is going to happen." By "something would happen" I meant that she would get sick. She usually did when she didn't get enough sleep. She was prone to bronchitis bouts, and she'd bark like a seal.

But, deep inside I knew that it had simply been "an accident." She would never take her own life. Beyond that, she would never have caused someone else's death on purpose. She would always go out of her way to go around, and wouldn't even run over a dead squirrel in the road. She'd never cause someone else's death.

I was still troubled by the nagging feeling that she hadn't tried to live because she knew how badly she was hurt, or because she knew that she had caused the death of two other people. I often wonder, had she lived, if she would have been able to live with herself, knowing that two others were dead because of something she did. When that thought would come to mind, I was almost thankful that she had died, too, for her mental and emotional sake.

CHAPTER SIX

"To every thing there is a season, and a time to every purpose under heaven: A time to be born, and a time to die;..."

Ecclesiastes 3:1 & 2a

Our lives were forever changed. Jenni died early Sunday morning, October 6, 1991, after being transported by ambulance to a Madison hospital. The surgeon had come out into the hall and met with us, telling us that they were going to be taking her into surgery, in hopes of getting the internal bleeding stopped. I remember asking him if they shouldn't be doing something about her skull. I knew that as the brain swelled, it could cause death. He told us that it was this way: If they didn't stop the internal bleeding, she was going to bleed to death. If the bleeding in the brain, and the swelling in the brain, weren't alleviated, she would die because the brain functions would stop, and her heart and lungs would cease to function, and she'd die. He made it very clear that any of her injuries were severe enough to cause her death, and he could make no promises. With that he turned and left to do the surgery.

When I saw him returning just a couple of minutes later, I knew my worst nightmare was about to become reality. He informed us that they were moving Jenni to the operating room, and on the way she had died. He said they had tried to revive her, to no avail.

She was never conscious after the accident. Nor did she ever breathe on her own. By never regaining consciousness, and the fact that both of the other people involved in the accident were already dead, the officers had no way of knowing what had actually happened to cause the accident. The sheriff's department had hoped that Jenni would be able to tell them once she came to. Now she was dead as well, and the answers to so many questions are forever unanswered.

There was no time for saying good-bye. We were only allowed in to see her for two minutes before they transported her by ambulance from Richland Center to Madison. I had asked if I could ride in the ambulance with her, but had been told that there really wasn't room. Our friends, Doug and Christy Duhr, drove us down, following the ambulance. I felt so helpless. I remember feeling so tormented by the fact that I hadn't been allowed to stay by her while she was dying. I saw no reason why, when they had to have known they probably weren't going to be able to save her life, they couldn't have allowed me to be with her. I was not allowed to be with her until she was dead. What good was that for her, or me, then?

Years later, the thing that helped me most to realize that I had to let go of the torment was the untimely death of my puppy, Cheyenne. She was such a smart pup. By the age of six months she had already learned many tricks. I adored her, and she adored me. We were inseparable. Then that fateful morning, August 22, 2003, when we were on our morning walk, she pulled out of her collar and ran across in front of a pickup truck. When she realized I was on the other side of the road, she tried to come back to me. The driver saw us every morning, and he always slowed down, but this morning he just assumed she was by me, and never saw her until I screamed as I saw his front wheel run right through the middle of her small body. I knew that she was seriously injured, even though the young man repeatedly tried to assure me she would be okay, as he sped us to the vet early that morning. Cheyenne lay on the passenger seat, with me crouched on the floor of his truck along side her. I was there in the vet clinic right alongside her, I had my hand on her as she lay on that table while the vet examined her, and I talked to her, trying to comfort her...but she died anyway about a half hour later. It was then that I realized that it wouldn't have made any difference if they had allowed me in by Jenni the whole time. Regardless of why or how it happened, the result was still the same, my puppy was dead, and so was my daughter. Even though that was not the natural order of things--a parent is not supposed to have to bury a child. That was still the way it was, and my being there would not have changed the outcome.

How like God, to use a puppy to give me this deep and profound understanding of my limitations at my daughter's death. And, how like modern-day doctors, with all their education and training, to snatch from their patients' families, the comfort and peace of being able to be at the side of their loved one as they are dying.

I'm sure I will experience a sense of loss and grief off and on my whole life. But, I know that God has a reason for everything that comes into our lives...and we don't always have the luxury of knowing the reason...we just have to operate on faith. If we knew all the reasons why, where would be the need of faith?

CHAPTER SEVEN

"In Rama there was a voice heard, lamentation, and weeping, and great mourning, Rachel weeping for her children, and would not be comforted, because they are not."

Matthew 2:18

After Jenni's death there were so many things to deal with. I suppose everyone deals with the death of their child differently. I know in our immediate family, the three of us handled it entirely differently. I can only tell you about me, as I don't know how my husband or son felt. Neither has ever really discussed much with me.

I walked around like I was in some kind of fog, going through motions. I didn't understand how every aspect of life could go on around me just as if nothing had happened. I carried a photo of her around in my hand for weeks so I wouldn't forget what she looked like.

I did things like send a letter to the hospital in Madison enclosing her graduation photos so they could see what she really looked like, since she had not been recognizable after the accident. Her whole body was so swollen from the trauma of the accident, as well as from the intravenous fluids and blood transfusions they had given her. She did not even faintly resemble the beautiful 18-year-old she was. I told them thank you for trying to save her.

We gave the money that was given to us as memorials to UW Richland and established a scholarship in Jenni's name. I typed out a sheet with Jenni's photo on it that I asked the university to give to the recipients of the scholarship each year along with the check. Yet another way I hoped to keep others from forgetting Jenni.

I went back to the hospital in Richland Center and asked to see her x-rays. They had given me her ring, earrings, and a necklace chain, but I knew she had been wearing a locket I had just given her for her 18th birthday, and it hadn't been among the belongings they had returned to us. I saw it on the x-ray, so I knew it hadn't been lost at the scene of the accident. After I had time to think about it, though, I was pretty sure that it would have just slid off the chain as they took it off her neck in the ER while working on her, and it probably had gotten thrown into the laundry with the sheets from the gurney, and lost forever. Although I checked with the hospital later, the locket was never found.

I asked the owner of the funeral home in Richland Center if he minded giving me a tour of his facility. I remember Jenni having told me that one of her classes in high school had taken a tour of the mortuary. I wanted to see where her body would have been taken, and what the process was to prepare her for burial. She knew from the tour. I wondered if that was why she had wanted to be cremated.

I spoke with her friends that had been on the ambulance crew that was called out that night to the accident scene. They were the ones who had worked so hard to keep her alive. They had gone out on the call, worked on Jenni, but because she was injured so severely, they didn't even know it was her. And not until they got back from the call were they told her name. Once they knew, they had even gone down to Madison after she was transferred.

I wrote to the ambulance crew and thanked them. We also donated money to them in memory of Jenni, to help them get more life-saving equipment.

I talked to her friend, Jenny Krueger, who had been the one that had gone to Madison with Jenni and Kevin that fateful night. She had a friend who had just gotten out of the Marine Corp, and she and Jenni thought it would be nice to double date, since Kevin had been a Marine, too, they would have something in common to talk about. They had driven separately, though, as she and Jenni weren't sure if either guy would be comfortable driving together. Plus,

37

Jenny and the young man had a lot of catching up to do, and would want to talk. By driving themselves, they could do that.

I wanted to know everything they had done that night. I wanted to know where they ate. I wanted to know that they'd had a good time. I wanted to know if she could shed any light on what might have happened.

I also went to the Sheriff's Department and looked through the photos of the accident that they had taken. I got copies of some of the photos; not sure why. I also got copies of the police report and witness statements of the people who had been following behind Jenni's vehicle, and who had seen the accident happen. Maybe I just needed photos and reports of the accident to confirm that it had really happened, because it seemed so unreal for so long.

My husband had gotten rid of the clothes Jenni had been wearing, because he did not want me to see their condition. They had kept her leather bomber jacket, though, that had been cut off her. Believe it or not, Jenni had told me once that she'd want to be buried in it. The funeral director cleaned it up as best he could and he just laid it in the coffin with her. Actually, she wanted to be cremated, she didn't want to be buried. I have felt badly that I didn't carry out that wish, but at the time I just couldn't bear the thought of having her cremated.

I had a teddy bear that an elderly friend had given me for my birthday years before, which Jenni had always wanted, but I had been reluctant to give her because it had been a gift to me. I had even gone so far as to buy her one that was the same size and color as mine. I put my bear in the coffin with her, and kept hers for me. I kept all of her things, and to this very day, have thrown little out. Every time we have moved, I've moved the boxes. I know that what is in them is of little earthly value, but I can't bear to part with the things that she had.

I put a small white wooden cross at the roadside where the accident happened. I found the very spot where something from the cars gouged a spot in the pavement, and small pieces of the cars that had fallen off as a result of the collision were still lying scattered about on the roadside.

We went to where our car was impounded out in a shed somewhere. I honestly can't even remember where it was now, or even much about looking at it. I don't even remember why we went. I do, however, remember the smell. It was a smell that hung with me for years afterward, as if it had been burned into my nostrils. It was a smell I can't even begin to describe...and won't even try to. I remember gathering up things that were scattered about the car...textbooks, papers and notebooks to name a few. I was obsessed with getting every last thing that Jenni had even touched...anything that had been a part of her life. It was as if I needed proof that she had existed.

At first I was just numb. I felt like I was living in a nightmare, and I kept hoping I would wake up. Hoping against hope that it was all just a bad dream. When that didn't happen, I started praying that, if I was ever able to go to sleep again, I would not have to wake up.

My chest physically ached, as though I'd been punched. It was as if I was fighting for every breath I took. Fighting against even taking another breath. I didn't want to keep breathing, but my body's natural reflex was to breathe, and so my chest hurt for a year or more. It felt like I had someone standing on my chest all the time.

Then, on the first anniversary of her death, I got a sharp stabbing pain in my chest. I prayed it was a heart attack, and as much as it hurt, the constant physical and emotional pain I lived with every day would be over, and I would be with her and Mom again. But, no such luck. The chest pain eventually passed. I think it was my heart trying to stop, but God wouldn't allow it.

For a long time I slept with a light on. Not sure why, but I didn't want it to be dark. Maybe because of Jenni's aversion to complete darkness. Maybe because, even though I knew it was only her body underground in the grave, I couldn't bear to think about how dark it would be, and how much she wouldn't like it that I had not had her cremated.

I didn't want to go to bed, but I didn't want to get up either. I didn't want people around me, but I didn't want to be alone. I didn't want to leave the house. I didn't want the radio or TV on, but I hated the silence. Nothing seemed right anymore.

I mentioned earlier that when Mom had died I felt abandoned and alone. Well, that was nothing compared to how I felt now that my child had died. I felt like God had abandoned me. I wondered where He was that night, and why He hadn't chosen to stop the accident, or, at the very least, miraculously spare her life. I'd heard stories of others for whom He had done just that, why not Jenni? I was angry at myself for feeling angry at God.

For years I couldn't bear the thought of meeting people because I knew how the conversation would eventually go. "So, do you have any children?" I vowed right away that every time that question was asked of me I was going to say, "Yes I do. Two. A daughter, Jenni, who would be such-and-such an age, but she died when she was 18 in a car accident, and a son, Dan, who is such-and-such an age." Inevitably, most people would then shy away from me, mumbling how sorry they were, or some such statement. I didn't care how uncomfortable the truth made them. I had no intention of just leaving Jenni out of the conversation, as if she had never existed.

The same is true about pictures of her. The fact that I have pictures everywhere of both my children makes some people uncomfortable, especially once they know Jenni is dead. But my thoughts on it are that I would not hide all her pictures if she had moved away to the east coast, as she had so often spoken of doing. Why should I hide them just because she died? She is still my daughter. I still love her, and I still want people to know she existed. I need to see the pictures, maybe for that same reason. I need to be reassured that she existed.

CHAPTER EIGHT

"And all his sons and all his daughters rose up to comfort him; but he refused to be comforted; and he said, For I will go down into the "grave unto my son mourning. Thus his father wept for him."

Genesis 37:35

As parents, we always want to be there to protect our children from any danger or harm. When an accident happens we feel almost responsible...even when we're not. I felt like I had really let Jenni down by failing to keep her safe. But, some things in life we have absolutely no control over, and accidents, obviously, are some of those things.

I spent a lot of time after her death trying to figure out how I could have kept it from happening, and how I could keep it from ever happening to Dan. If only I hadn't let her take the car that night. If only she had not decided to go on that double date a week earlier than originally intended. If only she had let Kevin drive, like she had told me she always did. If only, if only, if only. The "if only's" can drive you crazy. But the truth of the matter is that nothing I could have done could have kept the accident from happening.

The spring after Jenni died we decided to move back to Portage, where we had lived before moving to Richland Center. I really liked our historic house in Richland Center; we had poured so much of ourselves into restoring it. I swore I'd never move again. Between 1971 and 1986, we had moved nine times. I told John he would have to sell me with the house if he ever decided to move again. I wasn't planning on ever leaving, until they carried me out feet first. I always said it jokingly, but there was a lot of truth to my not wanting to move again. Another demonstration of how our plans don't always work out the way we think they are going to.

But, it seemed like a good idea to move back to Portage because John's dad, who we all affectionately call "Pa," had lung cancer and was not doing well. I really hated the thought of leaving the last place Jenni had ever lived, the last place we had lived together as a family. Yet, she had lived in Portage with us, so it was sort of like going home. It didn't really matter to me where we lived once we got there, because regardless of the house we bought, Jenni would never be there with us.

The move was made easier by the fact that I knew Pa needed us. So in February 1992, we returned to Portage and into the same apartment building where Pa lived. We did that so that we were near and could help him. He died in April of 1992, so I was happy that we were able to be there for him. However, John and I were not home when Pa died. It was almost like he planned it that way, to spare us the agony. It was the day we had to go back to Richland Center to close on the sale of our house.

After we moved back to Portage I was much closer to the cemetery in Pardeeville where Jenni was buried. I found myself spending every day there. I planted flowers at the gravesite and watered them, sometimes twice a day. They flourished, but my relationship with my son suffered. I tried to go to the cemetery while he was at school and my husband was at work. I told myself, I was not cutting into time I should be spending with them. Many days I spent the entire day at the cemetery. I even went in the middle of the night.

For years when it snowed I felt compelled to rush right over to the cemetery to shovel out a path to her grave, regardless of the time of day or night. I am sure most people who lived near the cemetery probably thought I had moved in over there. In fact, one time a former high school teacher of mine was out walking, and he stopped by to talk to me. He was wondering why I was always over there. No doubt a lot of other people wondered the same thing. Several times when I was there very late at night or in the wee hours of the morning, a police officer on patrol would swing into the cemetery to make sure there wasn't something going on that shouldn't be. I felt like a criminal when he asked for identification the first time, and inquired what I was doing there at that hour. Eventually I think he got used to seeing me there, and no longer stopped.

When my husband would suggest that we should move to Oxford to our lake cottage, I hated the thought of moving so far away that I couldn't go to the cemetery every day. It wasn't until our son Dan, (who lived in an apartment in our basement) married Melissa, they bought their own home and moved out that I was willing to go to Oxford. Empty nest syndrome I guess, but the day he moved out I told John I was ready to move. And we did.

CHAPTER NINE

"We are confident, I say, and willing rather to be absent from the body, and to be present with the Lord."

II Corinthians 5:8

It is strange how people react to you once you have a child die. Some people that you have known and been close friends with for years, and thought would be there for you through thick and thin, disappear from sight. Maybe it is that they just don't know what to say, when in reality, all you need is for them to be there, to listen when you're ready to talk...or just be there. Or, maybe it is that the realization that death is no respecter of persons, or age that frightens them. Maybe seeing it happen to someone they know, with children their children's ages, brings the reality too close to home.

I felt like I had contracted some horribly contagious disease that everyone was afraid they would catch if they got anywhere near me. That only added to my feeling of abandonment. Maybe it is because you are not the same after your child dies...and never will be again, and that makes them uncomfortable. Regardless of the reasons, I thank God that He provides others to come alongside in place of those who disappear from your life. I thank Him for those few who stay close to you as if nothing has changed.

I have countless cards that say, "Call me if you need to talk, or if there is anything that I can do to help." People who have had a child die will never call for help. My friend, Ruth (Lytle) Bahr, my best friend since high school, did something above and beyond that. She took off a week of work and came up from Omaha, NE, and stayed with me as soon as she heard Jenni had died, and she has always let me talk about Jenni, as does my dear friend, Anne Holets. Vicki

Bennett, who was at our house the weekend Jenni died, called me every couple of days for a whole year to check on me, even though I rarely felt like talking. Linda Hohl, a neighbor we had when we had lived in Portage before moving to Richland Center, made it a point to spend time with me after we moved back to Portage. She was literally one of the few who did, and I consider her to be one of my truest friends. By Ruth coming to be with me, Vicki calling me, as well as Anne and Linda spending time with me, it showed me that they did really care, and they weren't afraid of me, as so many others seemed to be.

It bothered me for a long time that people who knew us, and Jenni, were afraid to talk to me about her. It was as if they thought that if they didn't talk about her or say her name to me I wouldn't think about her. Or, if they did talk about her, it would make me cry. Little did they realize I never stopped thinking about her...and I cried anyway...maybe even more because they did not talk about her. I thank God for Peggy Pitts, a co-worker who let me talk, or cry, anytime I needed to.

I remember that one of the greatest fears I had right after Jenni died was that everyone would just forget her. I knew in my heart that that was not true. People who knew Jenni, who were friends of hers, would never forget her. But, that did not stop me from fearing that they would. I wish people understood that I longed for someone to talk to me about Jenni...to hear family and friends just say her name.

Maybe that desire comes from having Mom die so long ago that very few people who know me now ever knew her. And the people who knew her are in different circles now, and I do not often run into them. It is quite rare for me to meet someone who actually knew my mom. So, when it does happen, you can imagine how thrilled I am.

A couple years ago, after we moved to Oxford, WI, and I started working for an attorney, (he is, by the way, the same age as Jenni would be), his grandmother, Carolyn

Atkinson, who lives only three houses away from the office, shared a story about my mom.

One day when I was at Carolyn's house doing something for her, she told me that she just realized who I was. She asked me about who my folks were. I told her a little about them. She then asked me if I minded if she told me something about my mom and dad. I said I would love to hear anything she had to say regarding my parents.

Coincidentally, Carolyn had been in the same hospital room with my mom as Mom was dying. Carolyn relayed very touching memories to me of how loving my folks were, and how she had been so impressed by my dad. One time Mom had told him she was so hungry for a hamburger, and so he had run right out and gotten her one. But, best of all, she said, was a time when my mom had asked Dad to help her up out of bed. By that time, Mom was so weak she could not stand on her own anymore. She had wanted him to help her up, and to hold her for a minute, so they could hug. Carolyn told me that she could still see my dad so tenderly and gently doing just that.

It warms my heart when someone I've recently met tells me about something they remember about my mom. It lets me know she has not been forgotten. I feel the same way when someone shares memories they have of Jenni.

At first it really bothered me to hear people say they were sorry I had "lost" my daughter. I wanted to scream, "She's not lost. She's dead." Why do people have such an aversion to saying that word "dead"? I didn't "lose" my daughter. I was well aware of where she was…and where she wasn't. She was, after all, absent from the body and present with her Lord. I know they didn't mean any harm by it, but it seemed like such a horrible thing to say at the time.

I suppose it goes without saying that an equally strange question is, "How are you doing?" How is a person supposed to answer that question? Most people really wouldn't like, or know how to deal with, the answer, had I been truthful.

I struggled with how long I was in turmoil with the grief I felt. I even got to a point where I thought maybe if I weren't around, my husband and my son would be better off, because I was having such a hard time, while outwardly they seemed to be doing so much better than I. Even though I knew that everyone handles grief differently, it was very hard for me to be falling apart so visibly, while they appeared to be handling it so much better than I. I remember thinking they would be able to get on with their lives so much better if I were to just die and be done with it.

I struggled with how my inability to get back to life was affecting my son, whom I loved equally as much as I loved his sister. I wanted to be there for him, but I could barely get myself out of bed to face each day. I knew I was falling far short of the mom I wanted to be. I didn't want him to feel like he was not as important to me, and I added guilt to the feelings with which I struggled each day.

I struggled with how bad I felt about being a Christian, yet finding no comfort or peace in the fact that I would see Jenni again. I knew that she had accepted Christ as her Savior. She had written me from lab (a 3-week training program that teens went through to be able to work at Ft. Wilderness Camp in northern Wisconsin) in the summer of 1988:

> I am beginning to really feel like I know God better. Now it's as if He's more real to me and I'm becoming more aware of my desperate need to know Him better. Now, instead of wondering what I am going to do about my problems, I am starting to pray about them and to trust God to work things out.

I knew Jenni was in a far better place than she would ever be in here on earth. I knew she was in God's care, that she was feeling no pain, no sorrow, and she'd never be sick again. The horrible migraine headaches from which she had suffered her whole life, even when she was just a couple years old, were gone forever now. She was with the Lord,

47

and now nothing could harm her ever again. Nothing and no one could make her feel sad. But the selfish side of me missed her, and wanted her back here with me, even though I knew she wouldn't want to come back, even if she were given the opportunity. I kept thinking that something was wrong with me. I shouldn't feel so bad.

For years I cried in the shower so no one would hear me. I tried to make everyone, at least in my household, believe that I was doing okay, when I wasn't.

I put poems in the newspaper in Richland Center and Portage to commemorate her birthday and date-of-death each year, since she died. That is a part of my pursuit to keep her memory alive.

As I mentioned, I had placed a wooden cross next to the road where she had the accident. When we moved back to Portage, a neighbor who worked with metal made me a nice stainless steel cross that is there now. Each season I change how I have it decorated. I always stop by and put new flowers on Kevin and Mr. Wallace's graves, too, as well as sending two roses to the university campus with a card that says they are in memory of Jenni and Kevin. Once again, attempts by me to make sure people don't forget her.

I decorate her graveside for her birthday and for the different holidays. I remember trying to put lights on little Christmas trees, but our good old Wisconsin winters did not cooperate very well. The severe cold temperatures meant the batteries were short lived. Holidays are always hard, no matter how many years pass. However, the more that do pass, the more I realize that I have a harder time with the days and weeks leading up to the particular holiday or anniversary of her birthdays or death dates, than I do once the holiday actually arrives. I think maybe that is because I expend so much energy worrying about what it is going to be like again without her, that when it finally arrives I have no more emotion left to spend on the actual holiday. I can honestly say now, with my grandchildren here, I look forward to holidays again.

A person has to do what they have to do to make it through. I remember buying movies and watching them over and over. These are movies that Jenni had asked me to watch with her, or that she had told me she liked so well. I have ended up with quite a collection.

I listened to songs she liked. One of her friends had made me a cassette tape of songs she knew Jenni liked. One of the last songs that Jenni made me sit down and listen to with her was one that we played, and her brother sang, at her funeral. It is by The Escape Club, entitled "I'll Be There." The words are especially dear to me now, because the song was about a person who had died, leaving someone they loved very dearly behind, and it is as if that person who had died is telling the other that it is okay, and they aren't really gone, they are present everywhere. In the wind, in the new friends that are made, and that even though they have died, they are still very near. I find it very comforting that she felt such a connection with that song just before she died. And there was another song, one by Michael W. Smith, called "I Hear Leesha," which had rather the same subject matter. There he is talking about someone dear to him that had died.

Her friend, Ben Vincent, that she had seen while in New York with Jennifer Husnik, had sent me a copy of a videotape he had made while the two Jennifers were there that summer of 1991. I still watch it from time to time. I don't ever want to forget the sound of her voice.

Jenni had also done some video-taping of herself and friends a couple months prior to her death. I am grateful to God that she did that. At the time I remember worrying that she would lose or break the camera. I feel ashamed when I remember that now, because having the tape of some of her last days, seeing her having fun, means everything to me now.

Right from the very beginning I remember some sense of relief anytime anyone was willing to let me talk about Jenni. Talk about her, talk about the accident, talk about how much I love and miss her. They didn't have to say a word, they just had to listen. Those people were few and far between. Sometimes the only ones would be others who had gone through the same experience.

I was told about a group called Compassionate Friends, and meetings that they had. I attended off and on for quite some time. They are an organization that was formed for people just like me. People who had or were going through life after the death of their child, whether accidental, health issues, suicide, and even murder. Strange as it may seem, there was some comfort in knowing that I was not alone. There were others going through the same thing as I, and they were surviving.

Even though the result is the same, I can remember thinking that the only thing that would have been worse for me than how Jenni had died would have been if she had been murdered or had taken her own life. My heart went out to those who were trying to deal with those forms of death.

I remember reading lots of things on the grieving process once I could concentrate at all. I knew in my head that each person goes through the same basic steps, but at different rates and with different emotions, but it was still tough for me as I continued to have such a hard time handling Jenni's death, while outwardly my husband and son seemed to be moving on better. I knew it wasn't right, but I began to feel that they couldn't have loved her as much as I did if they could just pick up their lives and go on. It took me quite some time to get a grip on that whole situation.

Every year on Jenni's birthday I hike around Devil's Lake in the State Park over near Baraboo, WI. Jenni loved that park, and Dan often went there, too. I usually hike it with a friend, regardless of the weather. When the anniversary of the date of Jenni's death rolls around, I have always made plans to go somewhere. A friend or relative has generally gone with me. I have gone to see a lot of beautiful spots. Some waterfall tours, some natural beauty areas, some just places Jenni had told me about, and I had always planned to go see with her and never did. The past few years I am so grateful to my niece, Jessica Barltey, who stepped in and has gone with me. I wonder if she knows just how much it means to me that she takes time off work to spend it with me every year. I love her dearly for that, and feel like Jenni is looking down and smiling.

Years later after Jenni had died, when I must have appeared to Dan as if I were getting better, he told me that he had one of his teachers, just a few weeks after his sister's death, tell him that he needed to "get over it and move on." "After all," the teacher told him, "it has been several weeks now. Move on." I was glad that he had waited so long to tell me. I would have really had a problem with that. I will assume that particular teacher must never have had anyone die that was close to him, or he would never had said such a cold, thoughtless thing to my son.

How long the grieving process takes is different for each individual, and what works to help one, may do nothing to help another. Each person has to find what works for them.

For instance, the Compassionate Friends group. John and I both visited, but he only went once or twice. It wasn't for him, but it was very helpful for me to be able to talk with other parents who had suffered the death of a child. It really didn't matter the cause of the child's death, the pain was still there. The child was still gone.

There was a family in a neighboring town who knew one of our family members, and when she heard of Jenni's death, she wrote to me. She, too, had a teenage daughter die in a car accident years before. She and her husband actually had three children die in three separate car accidents several years apart. It was strange, though, because I remember thinking after Jenni died that now I was safe from any other tragedy. After all, one of my children was dead now as the result of an accident. That would never happen to me again. Dan was safe. However, after meeting this particular family, I knew that wasn't true. She had written to us a couple times, and we went to see them numerous times....mostly just to know that life could go on, when I sure didn't feel like I wanted it to.

When a parent dies, it is extremely hard, regardless of their age, but it is very different when your child dies. A part of you dies with them, and you are never the same.

When my child died, I lost a part of myself forever. As a woman, I had dreams of one day becoming a mother. Then the thrill of finding out I was pregnant. Feeling the first movement inside me. The morning sickness, which I had every day until Jenni was born. Nine months of having that little life inside me, forming into my child. What a miracle! What joy at her birth. Now, she had died so young. Not only was Jenni gone, but gone were all the plans and dreams we had for her future. They were gone because her life had ended so abruptly, without warning, and so tragically.

To me, Jenni was not only my daughter, a very part of me, but she was my friend. I thank God every day for the good relationship she and I had. I've often thought how horrible it must be for a mother to have a child die, and have had a bad relationship...how many regrets there must be. I'm not trying to say I didn't have any, I did. But the few I had made me thankful that I did not have to suffer the pains of regret over the lack of a good relationship with Jen.

After Jenni died in that car accident, I had years of sleepless nights, and so I started writing poems and writing in a journal to help me work through what I was feeling. I even wrote down everything I could remember about her so I wouldn't forget. Looking back in some of my journals of those early years, when I was writing long into the night and was getting very little sleep, the writing is barely legible. I felt like I was somehow communicating to her what was going on while she was gone. Almost like I was writing letters to her while she was away, until she would come home again. Obviously, I knew she wasn't coming home again, and I did know the only way I'd see her again would be when I, too, would close my eyes in death.

Only the promise of God that because of our faith in what Christ did for us on the cross, the way He provided for any person who would believe, kept me going. I knew Jenni had accepted Christ as her own Savior, and therefore, one glorious day, we would see each other again. I look forward to the day we will be reunited for eternity.

Now, every time I hear of someone who has had a child die, regardless of the cause of death or whether I know them or not, emotions and memories well up inside me. I liken how I feel to someone ripping the scab off the deep wound I have in my heart, and pouring salt in it. I know I don't know how they feel, only they do, but I know how I felt and how I struggled, and the thought of anyone having to go through that for the rest of their lives tears at my innermost feelings.

CHAPTER TEN

"I thank my God upon every remembrance of you."

Philippians 1:3

From time to time since Jenni's death I hear from friends of hers, or people who have a memory about Jenni, and have shared it with me. I want to share some of those treasured memories with you, in hopes it will help you better understand who Jenni was.

In case I failed to mention it before, Jenni had two friends whose names are also Jennifer. Don't think that didn't get confusing at times. We kept them separate by calling one Jennifer, one Jenny, and my daughter, Jen. Since then I have met another Jennifer, who I have grown very fond of through e-mail, and she spells her name "Jenni" just like my Jenni. She knew Jenni in high school, and I have been very blessed to hear from her, and hear memories that she is willing to share with me.

Jenni (Edwards) Andreae, the young lady who had gone to high school at Richland Center when Jenni was in school there e-mailed me:

> I have been thinking about you and your family so much over the years. I had known Jenni in high school. We had some art classes together with Mr. Beatty. She was a couple years older than I, so I was pretty excited that an older classman talked to me. We got along really well. I think about her often. I have stopped by her resting place whenever I'd be near Pardeeville. I have since moved out of the state and don't make it back to WI often.

I just wanted to let you know that your daughter is not forgotten. She was a very special person. You just never forget that kind of kindness. Her soft spokeness with a little bit of shyness is what I remember most, because I was too. That made her approachable.

I hope you are finding many more happy days now. I think of Dan and how he is a grown up now. I have not seen him since the funeral. It is amazing how time just never seems to stand still. But even though time does move forward, she is not forgotten. I hope your heart has healed some.

I better close for now. My name was Jennifer "Edwards", but my married name is Andreae. I go by Jen or Jenni. I was class of 1994 at RCHS to give you an idea of who I am...Judy. I have kept you and your family in my thoughts and prayers for many years now, and I will keep doing so.

She also e-mailed:

I miss Jenni. The world burned a little brighter with her here. I know we were not "hang out buddies", but she was just one of those people that were kind and wonderful and made you feel like you fit in. She didn't have to be nice to me. I was a dorky underclassman. Sometimes I read what she wrote in my yearbook. Jenni and I were in Theater Arts together and Mr. Beatty was our teacher. We were doing this Country Mouse Play. He made me wear this ugly stupid mouse get up. Oh, Jenni would laugh at my ears. They were not cute like Mickey Mouse, either. She helped me laugh thru my humiliation. She wrote about that in my year book. It was cute.

Jennifer Husnik, the young lady who Jenni had made the New York trip with right after graduation, wrote this not long after Jenni died. She now keeps in touch by e-mail, as she lives out in New Jersey:

Judy, I still think of Jenni EVERY day. I talk about her to everyone...they all know who she is, and know what a great friend she is. I feel her around me sometimes...mostly when I'm sad, stressed, or confused. She always plays her song on the radio for me....you know the one...right? It is only on when I really need it...and that tells me she is helping me get through certain things in my life. I also sometimes see her in people I meet. One person might laugh like her, or have the same gleam in her eye as she did...or even walk like her. It might sound crazy, but I do see her everywhere.

Another time she e-mailed me:

I'll be sending you some money like I always do to get Jennifer a red rose. I remember while we were in NY together she saw the roses on the street corner flower shops, and just loved them. She said "I would buy myself roses just to have them." Did you know it was on my 19th Birthday that I last saw her? I will always remember running into each other in Wal-mart that night. We spoke about how we needed to get together soon because we had gotten so busy with school since we came back from New York. I think that weekend she dropped off my Birthday card in my mailbox....I still have it. Honestly Judy...there is not a day that goes by that I don't think of her, or mention her to friends or patients. She is a very special person to me...and always will be.

Jacki Lingel was Jenni's first friend after we moved to Richland Center. I remember how thrilled she was to finally have made a real friend. It had been a move we had talked about with Jenni and Dan before their dad decided to take the job promotion to Richland Center with General Telephone. It was a job in management, after so many years of working just about every type of job for the phone company, and we were all excited. As a family we took a

56

road trip down to Richland Center to look around. The kids seemed really excited about moving at first. But by the time we finally moved, I think they both had changed their minds.

I think I made a bad decision when I suggested that we let them finish school in Portage, where we were living at the time, and wait to move until after the school year ended. It didn't take me long to realize that wasn't such a great idea. It probably would have been better to go down while school was still in session so that they would meet other kids and make friends. As it turned out, by moving in the summer after school was out, it ended up being a rather lonely summer for the two of them. But, like I said, when school started up in the fall, Jacki was Jenni's first friend.

Jacki e-mailed me:

> It's strange how even after 14 years I miss Jen so much. She is the only friend I have ever had who was/is my friend without expectations of me being anyone other than who I am. I hope you know how much she encouraged me (and well, I imagine all of her friends) to follow their hearts. She is a very special person. I hold everyone I meet to the standard she set for friendship. I know you must miss her incredibly every day of your life because I still miss her everyday myself. I think I have never told you how much of an impact she had on my life. Her friendship helped keep me sane and safe during a very unhappy time of my life. You know that I truly loved Jenni, love her still actually. You did a great job of raising her into probably the most accepting, loving, honest person that I have ever met, and the fact that she was like that before she even reached 18 is truly amazing. I wanted to share this with you.

Jenny Krueger was the young lady that Jenni had gone to Madison with the night of her accident. After the accident I asked her if she would write down what all they had done that night. I longed for any information about Jenni's last night, and Jenny graciously complied, although I know it was very hard for her. It took her almost ten months before she was able to write about it to me.

Jenny and Jenni hadn't become friends until after graduation. Jenny was a little older than my Jenni, but they met while working at a local grocery store in Richland Center, and became close in a very short time. She wrote:

> I miss her so much. I mean, we were only really good friends for a few months but it seems like I knew her forever – probably because we were together so much in that little time.
>
> Your little girl meant the world to me and she always will. No one will ever take her place in my heart.

A lady that Jenni had babysat for in Richland Center wrote me:

> Your family has always been so wonderful to me and my kids. You never treated us like we were less important than you, or that you were too good for us, no matter what situation we were in at the time. I loved Jen. She was one of the very few bright spots in my life after Chet moved us to Richland Center. She was the one person in the whole town that I could never wait to see. Your family was always everything I always wanted my family to be.

Corey Keller sent me a poem that he wrote about Jenni on April 6, 2006. It goes as follows:

BUTTERFLY

By Corey Keller

04/06/06

On that fateful Autumn day,
The angels from heaven swept you away.
There were unspoken words kept at bay,
So now I speak to your angel when I pray.
I have fond memories of you I hold,
They only bloom richer as I get old.
I remember the time when we shared a dance.
It was a brief moment of shy romance.
Your soft golden hair I forever cherish.
You're an angel in my heart that
    will never perish.
My heart will always skip a beat for you.
You were the rose no one else knew.
Like a flower garden in full bloom.
You were the diamond that captured the room.
Seeing your sunny smile made my eyes glow.
Your kindness was thick like fresh
    mountain snow.
If I could wish upon a falling star,
I would be the guiding light in that car.
Your dreams were so rich, like fertile ground.
Now they're wilted flowers without a honey bee
    sound.
As I gaze off into dark space,
I circle a star, there's your angel face.
Your spirit has risen into the blue sky.
Every Spring you return as a butterfly.

In a final exam essay from UW Richland, Jean
Birkett, a professor there, sent me a couple essays students
had written because they included something about Jenni.
The instructions were to, "in a well organized, accurate, and
clear essay, describe the single most significant learning
experience you have encountered this semester." One
young man wrote:

It started one day in the Symons Center. I was just sitting at a bench when I overheard two students talking (actually only one was a student, which I found out later.) They were just talking about going out later that week. I didn't actually catch much else or care; it was none of my business.

The thing I did notice was the girl, Jennifer Andres. I had talked to her, maybe twice, while playing pool a week before, so I just said, "Hi." She smiled and asked if my pool game was getting any better. I said no, and that was the extent of our conversation.

A week later I got the news that she and Kevin had both died. I felt a great loss, not for a close friend, but for someone who had a lot going for her and still was kind enough not to be a snob. I never knew Kevin.

I will miss the short-time friend of mine, and will always think of it as unfair that she died. From what I knew of her, she didn't have an enemy. If she didn't have potential, then no one did. Bye, and a few prayers, I guess that is all you can say.

Another student wrote, in response to the same instructions:

The single most significant learning experience I have encountered this semester was not a pleasant one: It was death. One person was a bright, beautiful, and loving young lady named Jennifer. The other was a husband and father to a close family friend. Both were taken in car accidents.

The accident itself is not important; it happened, and there is no way we can change that. What is important is that I have never really had to deal with anyone's death. Or more dreadful, is dealing with the family and friends that they left behind, and later asking yourself why, why did this have to happen.

Jennifer had everything going for her: she was smart, popular, and was so full of life. She was a friend, a classmate. Being a classmate (the same age) made her death so unreal. She was so young. I can't imagine having that short of time to live. Her family, knowing what a beautiful person she was, was torn apart. I could not tell them how sorry, how much I felt for them: no one could.

...What I learned from this horrible, but necessary experience, is that life is precious. I cherish my life and my family and friends. Because, before you know it, your life or someone you love, can be taken away. I will never forget Jennifer and Bryan, and what natural lesson they taught me.

September 6, 1991, one month to the very day before her death, Jenni wrote:

I hope I never forget how much the last four years have changed my life. In the last four years I met the person who will probably always be my best friend. It's because of her that I survived high school. I honestly don't know if I could have made it through without her, but I know one thing for sure, I'm glad I wasn't alone. Jacki left for college this fall in Illinois, and often before she left, we found ourselves remembering all the wild and crazy times we've shared. If it wasn't for Jacki, I never would have enjoyed anything in this town at all. I moved to Richland Center when I was 14. Needless to say, I hated it here. All I wanted to do was go "home," until the night of the first H.S. football game, where we met. A mutual friend introduced us, and we started to talk right away. The next thing we knew, the people we were with were no where to be seen.

Jacki and I seemed to form a sort of bond instantly. I'm not sure how or why really, but it was pretty clear to both of us that we would become the very best of friends.

Jacki and I went stag to homecoming our freshman year. It wasn't a whole lot of fun, but we went anyway. Jacki loved most social events, while I, of course, despised them. I was so afraid of people, especially ones I didn't know, but she didn't seem to mind it a bit. Eventually, I became the brave social one when I was trying to convince her moving to Illinois would be exciting.

Jacki represented the kind of person I wanted so desperately to be. She was so confident, so intelligent, that I sometimes felt a little inferior at first. She showed me that it's not that difficult to try new things. There are a lot of opportunities I might have passed up if it hadn't been for her encouragement and support. I think that's what means the most to me. I knew she would always be there for me. It didn't matter if she agreed with me or not. In fact, we felt differently about many issues, but I knew I wouldn't have to be alone. She said to me once, "I'll always stand by you; you might not get total agreement out of me, but I'll always be there." There were several rough times in our relationship, but no matter how bad things got, we knew we'd make it through. There were many nights we just talked things through, with laughter and tears.

One of her teachers, when writing a recommendation for Jenni for a scholarship she had applied for, wrote:

Jenni exemplifies the work ethic and moral values that we want all of our students to have when they leave Richland Center High School.

Jenni is a fine student and does earn excellent grades in her classes. The difference, though, between Jenni and many of the other excellent students, is that Jenni has to apply herself 100 percent of the time and not just rely on God-given ability. This is why I respect her so much! She is willing to go the extra mile, put in the extra time, ask the so-called "obvious" question, all in the pursuit of the knowledge and success that will help her attain all of her goals. I have never seen Jenni back down from a challenge that was worthwhile to pursue. Her work ethic is "top notch". Jenni is one of the three most hardworking and conscientious students I have ever been associated with in my 5 years in education.

Jenni is of high moral fiber. This, in part, comes from the outstanding job her parents have done in raising her. John and Judy are to be commended. But, parents can only offer the correct passage. It takes a strong independent person to take the lessons taught and apply them in today's always tempting world. Jenni has done this as well as any student I have ever been associated with. She not only knows "right from wrong", but she lives it!!! She is the kind of person I want to have as an example for our next generation, as we approach the 21st century. . . Besides being a quality student, more importantly she is a quality human being.

My grandson, bless his little heart, even talks about his "Aunt Jenni." He only knows her from the photos that his mom and dad have around their house. He'll tell me, "Nana, I have an Aunt Jenni, but she's dead." I smile and say, "I know you do, Benji, and she'd love you very much if she could meet you." And he usually replies, "She's in heaven, so I can't see her."

I always feel good that he'll talk about Jenni, even though he doesn't know her. But at the same time, I feel sad that she's not here to be a part of his and Lily's lives. She is a part in some ways. Dan and his wife, Melissa, named Lily after Jenni, by naming her, Lillian Jennifer Andres. That meant a lot to his dad and me.

I still hear from several of Jenni's friends now and then. Each time that I do it warms my heart to know that she has not been forgotten, nor will she ever be by those who know and love her.

CHAPTER ELEVEN

"For God so loved the world that He gave His only begotten Son, that whosoever believeth in Him should not perish, but have everlasting life. For God sent not His Son into the world to condemn the world, but that the world through Him might be saved..."

John 3:16-17

A dear friend told me, "There's more to a person's life than that dash on the headstone between the date they were born and the date they die. It is what they do with their life in between that really matters."

I remember my mom always repeating the saying, "Only one life, 'twill soon be passed. Only what's done for Christ will last."

Our pastor, Levi Snyder, who co-officiated at Jenni's funeral, always says, "You never see a U-Haul behind a hearse."

I think the meaning of those statements rings so true. We can waste our lives here on earth, accumulating things. Things that we can't take when our mortal bodies go to the grave. The only thing we can take with us into eternity are the souls of family, friends, and those with whom we have shared the Gospel message. Those who have come to a saving knowledge of the Lord Jesus Christ. Or, we can waste our lives wallowing in grief, and be rendered useless to be of any help to others.

We need to share the Gospel message with all we meet. The Gospel message can be summed up pretty simply. So simply, in fact, that even a child can understand and accept it by faith. Our pastor always says, "We are saved by grace alone, through faith alone, in Christ alone." There is nothing anyone can do to merit salvation. No works we can do are good enough to secure us a place in heaven. It is not by means of anything that we have done, but it is only by His grace and mercy that we can spend eternity in Heaven.

There are a few verses in the Bible in the book of Romans that plainly lay out the way to everlasting life. Some people refer to it as "The Roman Road." It sets forth the basic steps for the plan of salvation that God provided, through His Son, Jesus Christ.

First, a person has to realize that they are lost and sinful. Romans 3:23 says, "For all have sinned and come short of the glory of God." All means just that. No one is righteous, not even one person.

The penalty for that sinfulness is death, according to Romans 6:23. "For the wages of sin is death, but the gift of God is eternal life through Jesus Christ our Lord."

But while we were in our sinful state, according to Romans 5:8, "...God commendeth His love toward us, in that, while we were yet sinners, Christ died for us."

Romans 10:13 goes on to explain, "For whosoever shall call upon the name of the Lord, shall be saved." We do this by admitting to ourselves and to God that we are sinners. Romans 10:9 tell us, "That if thou shalt confess with thy mouth the Lord Jesus, and shalt believe in thine heart that God has raised Him from the dead, thou shalt be saved.

Once a person has accepted Christ as their own personal Savior, Paul tells us in Romans 12:1-2, "I beseech you therefore, brethren, by the mercies of God, that you present your bodies a living sacrifice, holy, acceptable unto God, which is your reasonable service. And be not conformed to this world: but be ye transformed by the renewing of your mind, that you may prove what is that good and acceptable and perfect will of God."

One thing that I find comfort in regarding Jenni's funeral was that there were some who heard the Gospel message at her funeral who may never have heard it otherwise. Her death made a lot of young people think about life, and the end, thereof, and what there is after death. If only one person came to a saving knowledge of Christ because of Jenni's death, I would feel it had not been in vain.

CHAPTER TWELVE

"...weeping may endure for a night, but joy cometh in the morning."

Psalms 30:5

I smile when I think of just how far I've come over the years since Jenni's death in 1991. Even though I will never be the same, I feel as if I have finally found my "brighter tomorrow." I have two beautiful grandchildren, Benjamin (Benji) Isaac Andres and Lillian (Lily) Jennifer Andres. Both are the joy of my existence, and they keep me looking for the good in each day I am given by God.

I do silly things, too, like when we got our new puppy, the one I picked out had a white spot on the back of her head. I said it was because Jenni had looked down from heaven when they were born, kissed her fingertips, touched the back of the head of the puppy she felt was the one I should take, and it bleached the color out of the spot she touched. Silly, I know, but it made me feel good to include her in the process of choosing my puppy. Both Cheyenne and Shiloh, the puppy I got after Cheyenne's death, have that same white spot. I know, it sounds a little crazy, but I think its okay, as long I don't truly believe that is what happened. It just made me feel good to think of it that way. I called it, "Cheyenne's angel kiss."

Another example that I feel demonstrates that I have turned the corner to the brighter tomorrow is that a friend, Cindi Umstad, recently had written a song for her mother-in-law's funeral, and I was so moved by the words that I asked her if she minded if I changed some of the words slightly and sang it in honor of Jenni's birthday this past year, 2005. Jenni's birthday, May 29th, fell on a Sunday in 2005. She graciously agreed, and even came and played her guitar for me to sing it. (A copy of the words are in

Appendix A because Cindi so graciously gave me permission to print the words.) I guess the fact that I could sing it shows just how far I have come down the road to a brighter tomorrow.

I have found, too, that being a "Big Sister" to a "Little Brother" in the Big Brother/Big Sister Program has been very rewarding and helpful to me. Roman Bundy has been my Little Brother since he was ten years old. He just turned seventeen this year. I can honestly say that the time I've spent with Roman has probably helped me as much, or more, than it has him.

Since Jenni's death, I have shared some of my poems with friends, and many of them have encouraged me to write my story and get it and my poems published. They told me they thought it might be helpful to others who have gone or are going through the same ordeal. That is the reason that this book has now come to fruition. If heeding their advice results in helping even one person as they travel down their own road to recovery from grief, I will be thankful and feel like this endeavor has been worthwhile.

The following poems are the fruits of all my sleepless nights. I am sharing them now with others in hopes that maybe through them someone may find some comfort as they follow my journey through the valley of the shadow of death; through the dark days of grief...to a brighter tomorrow. My hope is that the story of my journey, and the poems I have written in an effort to express what I was feeling, may help someone work through the pain they live with everyday since the death of their child, and that they, too, will be able to find a brighter tomorrow.

POEMS FROM MY HEART

Written by
Judy A. Andres

From
1991
through
2006

In Loving Memory of
JENNIFER LYN ANDRES

05/29/73 to 10/06/91
19TH Birthday – May 29, 1992

Jen, you'd be 19 Friday, May 29, 1992. This is so different from your last birthday. I never dreamed your 18th would be your last. I don't suppose birthdays are celebrated in Heaven, but just in case you can have this message, I want you to know that I love you and miss you as much today as I did the day you died. Love, Mom.

I also included the inscription that is on the back of Jenni's gravestone ~ it was in one of the sympathy cards that someone sent us:

Time cannot steal the treasures
that we carry in our hearts,
Nor ever dim the shining thoughts
our cherished past imparts,
And memories of the ones we've loved
still cast their gentle glow
To grace our days and light our paths
wherever we may go.

MISSIN' YOU

By Judy A. Andres
May 1993

Your bright blue eyes, and radiant smile ~
Your laughter, and your tears.

Sure am missin' you!

Our long talks in confidence,
On happenings, and on your fears.

Sure am missin' you!

Unfulfilled plans ~
Unfulfilled dreams ~
Your future ~
All those unclaimed years.

Forever missin' you!

PICKING UP THE PIECES

By Judy A. Andres
September 14, 1993

Picking up the pieces
Of my shattered life.
Days of endless sorrow~
Of confusion, and of strife.

Struggling with my emotions,
To get them under control.
Days of great frustration
To mold me back to whole.

Changed, forever different~
Yet shadows of the same.
Outward a strange resemblance.
Inward forever in pain.

OCTOBER

By Judy A. Andres
September 14, 1993

It steals the warmth of summer now
As it stole the life from you.
It creeps in and steals away
All that spring and summer grew.

It has taken part of the sunshine
That made my life worthwhile.
It has shattered all my hopes and dreams,
Left me feeling like an abandoned child.

It has stolen my sense of security.
Left me weary, and so full of doubt.
Wondering if we can control anything . . .
Wondering just what life's all about.

Yet after October, comes winter,
With its icy winds that blow.
Covering the death of the summer
With a blanket of new-fallen snow.

Everything living lies dormant ~
Awaiting the freshness of spring.
When the earth is again clothed with beauty
That only things living can bring.

TO MY SON

Love Mom
September 14, 1993

There are times, I'm sure, it seems
I've left, never to return.
I'm sure you too feel abandoned ~
For a normal life do yearn.

I want you to know, I'm trying.
I love you the same as her.
I want you to know that I'd be feeling the same,
Had it been you, instead of her.

You mean more to me than life itself.
You both do, and that is true.
And so there's one thing that I want you to know ~
I'm still here, and trying, because of you!

Photo taken by Nelson Photography in
Richland Center, WI

In Loving Memory
JENNIFER LYN ANDRES

05/29/73 to 10/06/91

Everything now seems such a mess ~
Our lives have changed so much.
No more to have your presence here ~
Nor ever to feel your touch.

I'm trying to be strong and brave ~
I'm trying to get by.
To do just as you told me to. . .
And trying not to cry.

I suppose I should be happy,
For all the good times that we shared.
I really have so few regrets,
Because you knew how much I cared.

But a selfish voice within me screams,
"Please give her back to me!"
Because there's so much hurt and pain
In each precious memory.

You lived your life so full, so fast,
Never taking time to rest.
Places to go, and things to do ~
Always trying to be the best.

I really wish someone could tell me
Just how long this grieving will take.
I long to remember your radiant smile,
To think of you without feeling my heart break.

It seems so unfair to have lost you~
With no warning, no time for good-bye.
But, Jen, if love alone could have kept you here,
I'm certain you'd never have died.

Some tell me, "Time heals all sorrow."
Others say, "Time will help you forget."
But time, so far, has only proved
How much I miss you yet!

QUESTIONS

By Judy A. Andres
10/18/93

As a young child we question
The "whys" of everything.
We drive our parents crazy
With all the questions that we bring.

Sometimes they have the answers
Our inquiring minds satisfy.
So we move on and run and play
"till something else leaves us mystified.

Oh, that adult worlds were as simple,
And answers as easy as pie,
But tragedy has left us here
Forever questioning "Why?"

SOOTHE THE HURT AWAY

By Judy A. Andres
10/18/93

I was almost always there
When you'd fall and skin your knee,
To pick you up, and hug you tight,
And soothe the hurt away.

The days rolled by...There came the time
When hurt ran deeper still,
Within your heart and in your mind,
Making the role as soother much harder to fulfill.

But I was there to listen,
To all the woes you told.
Sometimes still to hold you, or cry with you,
To try to soothe the hurt away.

Now that's forever over.
No more hurt for you, nor pain.
Your hurt's been soothed forever ~
Leaving behind a never ending pain!

UNTITLED

By Judy A. Andres
10/19/93

Days are seemingly endless.
Countless hours pass me by.
Time seems but an illusion.
I ask myself, "Why try?"

But then I look around me,
At the blessings given me.
I see my son and husband,
And ask, "How can it be?"

How can it be with all I see
That I should hurt so bad?
I need to keep my eyes on them,
Not what I could have had.

We cannot always see His plan,
Nor will we all agree.
We have only to believe,
He knows what's best for me.

A STRANGER IN OUR HOUSE

By Judy A. Andres
10/19/93

There is a stranger in our house
Since you went away.
No one knows quite who she is,
Or if she's here to stay.

She bears a strange resemblance
To one they knew before,
But she's so very different,
So they try hard to ignore.

They seem to be afraid of her,
Tho' I dare say she's no threat
To anyone, or anything.
She hasn't harmed them yet.

She seems so very quiet now.
Preoccupied at best.
I hear tell she stays up late,
And finds it hard to rest.

She's kept alive with memories,
Yet tortured by the same!
Hoping soon to be woke up,
Yet knowing nothing's changed.

The joy of life seems drained away.
She's solemn and forlorn.
And finds it hard to face the day ~
Each and every morn.

Do you recognize her?
Her heart's been torn in two.
The closer that I look at her
I see me without you!

PICTURING MEMORIES

By Judy A. Andres
10/19/93

I gaze into your clear blue eyes
And wonder if you see
The memories of days gone by
When you were here with me.

Those days seem now so long ago ~
Yet sometimes oh, so near.
I picture them within my mind ~
And hold them all so dear.

God surely gives us memories
To help us through our grief.
They come to spend some time with us
To give us some relief.

Relief from all the heavy weight
And burden that we bear,
In living life without you now,
While you are in His care.

MOVING DAY

By Judy A. Andres
10/21/93

Where is JOY that filled my heart?
Why has she gone away?
Was something done to scare her off
That cold October day?

And where is PEACE?
He left with JOY ~ and LONELINESS moved in.
Oh what a shambles he did make.
It's really quite a sin.

ANGER wasn't far behind,
His ugly head to rear,
To add to my confusion
And I began to fear.

GUILT came right up to my door
And begged to come in, too.
I thought awhile, but then replied,
"I have no time for you!"

"Take your accusations.
Take them far away ~
And LONELINESS and ANGER, too."
I must not let them stay!

For if I do I know that they
Will only cause more pain
For others here beside me,
Who want me back again.

THROUGH FAITH, BY GRACE

By Judy A. Andres
10/21/93

There are some things in this old life
We may not understand.
But that's no cause for doubt or fear ~
Don't let go of His hand!

He has not left us comfortless.
He shares all of our grief,
And longs for us to yield to Him
And feel an inward peace.

A peace that only He can give,
Whatever comes our way.
We've only to remember this,
And not forget to pray.

Please help me Lord to trust you
When the future seems so bleak.
Help increase my faltering faith,
For I am oh so weak.

Lift me up, and hold me,
'Till I can stand alone.
Help me keep my eyes on You,
And not on all my woes.

Until we're all together,
And in a better place,
Help me always to remember
I've been saved through faith, by grace.

IN THE QUIET

By Judy A. Andres
10/21/93

In the quiet of the night
When everyone's asleep,
I sit here with my memories
And try hard not to weep.

I think of all the fun we had.
I think of sad times, too,
When you would come to me to talk,
In hopes I'd know what to do.

You trusted me for answers
To the perplexing things in life.
I miss all of those special times ~
Will miss them all my life!

Nothing can change what's happened,
Nor will my love grow cold.
I'll treasure all the memories.
They'll keep helping me, even when I'm old.

TORN IN TWO

By Judy A. Andres
10/21/93

Half of me's been torn away
While half of me's still here
To face the future, come what may,
Year after year.

Half of me longs to follow you.
The other half begs me to stay.
Sometimes I'm uncertain
Which half will have its way.

It takes two halves to make me whole
So I long for the day
When we'll be reunited and
Together, forever we'll stay.

JUST WONDERING

By Judy A. Andres
10/21/93

I can't keep from wondering
What you'd be doing now
Had you been granted a long life
In this ole' world somehow.

Would you be going far away,
Attending college, too,
The way I watch so many kids,
And some of your friends do?

Or had you found that one true love,
And would the plans be laid
For Dad to give the bride away
On that your wedding day?

Would we still be doing things
That mother/daughters do?
Would you still find time for me,
And would I, too, for you?

Would you want me there with you
When your first child was born?
I know I'd want to be there
Whether it was night or morn.

I guess the "Would have," "Could have,"
"Should have beens,"
Can never come to be.
So, I should lay them all to rest,
And concentrate on those still here with me.

MEMORIES

By Judy A. Andres
11/08/93

Your memory keeps haunting me
No matter what I do.
Everywhere I turn I seem
To see a bit of you.

There are so many places
That we have gone before.
So now no matter where I go
Reminders knock at Memory's door.

I took you there ~ We went there, too,
So often as a child.
You liked that place ~ That one scared you ~
Or, there you just went wild.

So may precious memories
Of songs I sang for you.
Or stories that you had me read~
Even made up one or two.

And songs I hear upon the air,
Or movies you had me watch.
So many things I do recall ~
I hope they never stop.

For all I have are memories
Of you~ things you did and said.
And if there were no memories ~
You really would be dead.

88

JUST WANTED YOU TO KNOW

By Judy A. Andres
11/08/93

I sit sometimes and wonder
Was this really meant to be?
Was it something done, or something said
That caused this great catastrophe?

It seems quite strange, almost absurd
That this could be His plan...
To give you life, then snatch you back
In such a short span.

You had barely started living
When He came and took you home.
Had not the chance been given yet
To be out on your own.

You were looking forward yet
To all that life might bring.
Wondering what it held in store ~
Anxiously awaiting everything.

Seemingly so full of life
On that October day.
How was I to know that He
Was calling you away?

There was no way of knowing.
I suppose that's for the best.
For how would anyone prepare
To stand this awful test?

If I had known what I know now,
I'd have never let you go.
I love you more than life itself ~
Just wanted you to know.

LIFE

By Judy A. Andres
11/19/93

Life is so uncertain,
Or so we have been told.
We cannot know the length of it,
Or how it will unfold.
It's not how long we're given
That makes the difference ~
But rather what we do with it ~
How we withstand its tests.
Will they make us bitter ~
Or strengthen us instead?
To help us be the very best
With time that we have left.
For bitterness and anger
Waste the precious gift of life.
They leave us wallowing in pity,
In confusion, full of strife.
So, since life is for the living,
And not for those now dead...
We need to make the most if it ~
Not wasting it instead.

THE STORM

By Judy A. Andres
11/19/93

Inside my soul there rageth
A storm so fierce and bold,
It threatens to capsize my ship,
To batter all it holds.
I see the waves about me,
And gaze trembling in fear.
They crash in all around me,
Destroying that which I hold dear.
Dark angry clouds surround me.
They draw ever nearer.
And though I try hard not to yield,
My heart is filled with fear.
The angry skies are threatening
To plunge me to despair.
The jagged rocks keep beckoning
Me come into their snare.
T'would be so easy to give up,
To sink in deep despair.
To let the waves engulf my life ~
I wouldn't even care.
Except I keep remembering
Some of the last words that you said,
"You'd need to go on living, Mom,
Even if I were dead."

REST ON HIS PROMISES

By Judy A. Andres
12/06/93

Although you're gone now from my sight
I needn't fret nor fear,
For God is faithful to His own,
And He is ever near.

His promise He has given,
He is faithful to the end.
He will never ever leave us ~
On that we can depend.

Even though at times it seems
As though He's far away,
I still will take Him at His Word
And turn to Him and pray.

He knows just how I'm feeling,
For He's felt the same things too,
When He chose to become a man,
And gave Himself for me and you.

And so I'll lean upon Him,
Since I cannot stand alone,
And rest upon His promises
'Till we meet at His Throne.

FREE AT LAST

By Judy A. Andres
12/06/93

Time seems like a prison now ~
And death, it holds the key
That will unlock the chains that now
So heavily burden me.

I anxiously await the time
When death will come to call ~
Informing me my times run out,
And I have used it all.

Then my imprisoned soul will rise
In jubilant ecstasy.
T'will be time for rejoicing
For at last I will be free!

UNDERSTAND?

By Judy A. Andres
Started 12-1993
Finished 01/05/94

Life's like an elusive dream
On which I can't depend.
I do not know the path it takes,
Nor what's around the bend.

I only know that come what may,
It's all part of His plan.
He knows just what's best for me,
I need not understand.

I may not see it clearly now,
But there will come a day,
When all the cares and woes down here
Will all be passed away.

HOW I LONG FOR THAT DAY!

DEATH ~ FRIEND OR FOE?

By Judy A. Andres
01/05/94

"There's two sides to every story" ~
That saying is quite old.
The day DEATH came and claimed you,
I counted him my FOE!

BUT ~

When DEATH comes and calls for me,
And all my pain will end,
I will, at last, look up and say,
"DEATH has become my FRIEND."

REUNION

By Judy A. Andres
01/10/94

Oh to have you back again ~
But that will never be,
Until we meet that glorious day,
For all eternity.

The trump will sound, the dead will rise,
And then my eyes shall see,
We that yet are alive, and here,
Caught up to be with thee.

The day, the hour, we cannot know,
So we'll wait impatiently,
In hopes the time will not be long,
'Til we're again a family.

TREASURES

By Judy A. Andres
01/10/94

I have two precious treasures,
Far exceeding gems or gold.
T'were given me by God above,
To nurture and to hold.
He knew their value far outweighed
The trials they might bring.
He knew I'd never trade them ~
No, not for anything.
For there is nothing could replace
The joys that they do bring.
And memories of days gone by
Still cause my heart to sing.

COLOR CHANGE

By Judy A. Andres
Started 01/14/94 - Finished 01/17/94

As I sit and ponder,
The years that have gone by,
So many thoughts come back to me,
And tears well in my eyes.

I remember you both little ~
I felt needed, oh, so much,
When you were ill, or scared, or hurt,
You were comforted by my touch.

Or, when problems seemed perplexing,
Whether they were big, or small,
You'd come to me, we'd talk them out.
I listened to them all.

Each moment was so precious.
Too soon you both were grown.
I watched the transformation
As you each became your own.

I knew that day was coming,
As I felt you pull away,
To be a person all your own ~
I dared not stand in your way.

The love we had between us,
Seemed ever changing day by day,
And I began to feel as though
I now was in the way.

It made me feel so useless,
Yet I know that isn't true.
It's just my role as mother
Was taking on a different hue.

THE MAKING OF A MAN

By Judy A. Andres
01/17/94

There was a time when you were but
A twinkle in my eye.
I had so many plans and dreams ~
I knew we had to try.
For there was yet a life unlived ~
One that was meant to be.
A precious life, a miracle ~
T'would be a part of me.
It wasn't long and I could feel
A flutter deep within,
As you began to form and grow ~
I knew all hearts you'd win.
Your sister waited anxiously
For when you'd come "to play"
And was slightly disappointed when
You couldn't play with her right away.
We were so proud, a baby boy!
Two weeks earlier than doc had said.
You snuck in just past midnight,
And kept us all from bed.
So often sick, you couldn't breathe ~
I'd sit and hold you tight.
You and blankie'd cuddle close ~
I'd hold you through the night.
Yet, you always seemed so happy ~
Easy-going, you took life as it came.
Not much seemed to bother you,
Your big brown eyes sparkled just the same.

It seemed all of a sudden though
That you began to grow ~
From child, to teen ~ a scary thing,
As every mother knows.
But now it seems like overnight
You've grown into a man,
And I just want to tell you, Dan,
I'm glad you're the son I had!

I MISS YOU

By Judy A. Andres
01/28/94

I miss you every morning
As I wake to face the day,
And search for strength to see me through
Somewhere along the way.

There's not a moment passes by
That you're not on my mind,
And with the passing of each day,
New memories unwind.

I miss you throughout all the day.
Yet, when the day is through,
And evening casts its shadows tall,
I still am missing you.

I struggle so within my soul
To understand the "Why?"
That He should call you home to Him,
And leave me here to cry.

I miss you as the sun sinks low,
And sets the sky ablaze,
In colors, vibrant the hue ~
I'm really quite amazed.

To think that God can paint the sky
In such a grand array.
How can I help but trust in Him
Until my dying day?

And so I go on living.
Yet when my life is through,
I know that I will smile and say,
"I'm glad that I had you!"

THE ROAD

By Judy A. Andres
01/31/94

There is a road to travel
For each and everyone.
The path may lead to joys untold,
Or joys may vanish one by one.
I know not where each path will lead,
But I'll trudge ever on,
And take the good, along with bad,
And give thanks to God's Son.
For He is here beside me,
No matter come what may.
He's promised I can lean on Him ~
He'll help me through each day.
Yes, there'll be times when I will feel
Unable to go on ~
And all my strength seems drained away,
And hopelessness abounds.
Yet He has not forsaken me.
It's all part of His plan.
He gently lifts me close to Him,
And firmly holds my hand.

THE END OF TIME

By Judy A. Andres
01/31/94

The LONLINESS your absence yields

Is with me FOR ALL TIME.

The PAIN I feel within me

Lessens not with PASSING TIME.

The HOLLOWNESS within my heart

Shall be there FOR ALL TIME.

The EMPTINESS, no longer filled

Is changeless with the TIME.

So I know I'll be MISSING you,

Until the END OF TIME!

LOVE IS...

By Judy A. Andres
01/31/94

Love is...

Taking the good times

Along with the bad.

Reflecting more on the

Fun times you've had.

Saying, "I'm sorry,"

When you know that you're wrong.

Being there for the other

When they're not feeling strong.

Thinking more of the other

Than you do of yourself.

Sometimes putting your wants

Back up there on the shelf.

Taking time out to say,

"I appreciate you!"

For love's not just words ~

But more what you do.

THE GREAT INJUSTICE

By Judy A. Andres
02/02/94

It seems so utterly unjust
The pain I feel inside,
Each time a memory of you
Is called back to my mind.

The times we had that brought such joy
Now bring me twice the pain.
I search for solace in my thoughts,
But the searching in is vain.

All the things we used to do
Can n'er be done again.
And things done now are shadowed
By your absence, and seem grim.

And that is why it seems so cruel
Such joys should now cause pain.
Your parting left such sorrow,
Why should your memories cause such pain?

WE USED TO

By Judy A. Andres
02/02/94

We used to sit and watch the sun
As it set in the west.
We used to watch the sunrise, too ~
It's hard to choose which one was the best.
We used to go and take long walks
Or ride our bikes around.
We used to sit in our porch swing
And gaze down towards the town.
We used to sit and watch movies,
Or talk of books we read.
We used to scratch each other's back
When it was time for bed.
We used to talk a lot about
The things that made us sad.
We used to talk a lot about
The things that made us glad.
We used to cry together,
But now I cry alone.
For everything we "used to do"
I now do it alone.

MY TEARS

By Judy A. Andres
02/07/94

There is a never-ending pain
Deep within my heart.
Relentless, never ceasing ~
Since you did depart.

An emptiness now lingers
Every waking hour.
Nothing can ever fill it ~
It's within no one's power.

Time seems to play the cruelest tricks,
As memories float by.
At times it seems like yesterday,
Yet I know that's a lie.

Other times it seems as though
You have been gone for years.
And so I sit and sort it out,
As my eyes fill with tears.

Tears that say, "I love you."
My tears say, "I'm so sad."
Tears that say, "I'm lonely,
And I'm feeling, oh, so bad."

My tears flow o'er the good times,
As well as o'er the bad.
They pour out for the times we've lost ~
The one's we'll never have.

I think those are the saddest,
For they will never be,
Because you have been taken young,
And are no longer here with me.

BRIGHTENED DAYS

By Judy A. Andres
02/11/94

I've watched you grow from little on ~

Both are my pride and joy.

I felt the luckiest on earth

To have a girl and boy.

No joys on earth could e'er compare

To joys you both do bring.

The love that's shared between us

Goes far deeper than anything.

For children are a part of you

In oh, so many ways.

And every step along the way

They brighten up your days.

REFLECTIONS

By Judy A. Andres
02/11/94

Reflections of the days gone by
I see where e'er I gaze.
In faces of the passers by ~
Or in the evening's haze.
It seems no matter where I look,
No matter what I do,
Someone smiles the way you smiled,
Reminding me of you.
Then someone laughs the way you laughed,
Or wears the clothes you'd wear.
Or combs their hair the way you did,
And has skin just as fair.
Or I'll look up and see your eyes ~
Sometimes gray or blue.
Or smell the perfume that you wore ~
Reminding me of you.
The world now is a mirror,
Or so it seems 'tis true.
For everywhere I turn I see
Reflections there of you.

WATCHING, WAITING...

By Judy A. Andres
02/12/94

I used to sit and watch the clock
As it passed nine, then ten.
Eleven, and at last midnight ~
Soon you'd be home again.
I'd sigh a sigh of great relief
As you walked through the door.
I knew you never understood
What I was waiting for.
It wasn't that there was no trust
Between us. Don't you see?
I had to know that you were safe.
Yes, safe back home with me.
So many things can happen,
O'er which we've no control.
Accidents that claim a life,
And tear deep at the soul.
Your death was such a tragedy.
It was a two-fold one.
Not only taking you from me ~
But me, too, from my son.
For though I'm here in body,
Half of me left with you.
I try to be the mom to him
That I was for you.
And though I know I fall far short,
I hope when he's a dad,
He will look back at me and say,
"Mom, now I understand."

LIFE GOES ON

By Judy A. Andres
02/13/94

The sun comes up,
A new day dawns ~
    And life goes on.

People hurry
To their jobs ~
    And life goes on.

The rain, the sleet,
The snow doeth fall ~
    And life goes on.

A life is formed, and lives,
Then dies,
    And life goes on.

Every single day, somewhere,
Someone's child dies ~
    And life goes on.

My heart was broken
When you died ~
    And life went on.

I longed to follow
After you ~
    And life went on.

I feel as though
I've died inside ~
Yet life goes on.

The sun comes up,
A new day dawns ~
AND LIFE GOES ON.

LIFE'S NOT FAIR

By Judy A. Andres
02/22/94

"Life's not fair!" I'd always say
When you would come to me,
With some injustice in this world
That you'd so plainly see.

I hoped that you'd both come to learn,
No matter how well planned,
There would be times here in this life
That you'd not understand.

I wanted both of you to know that,
Even though not fair,
There was a lot of good in life.
Just look, you'd find it there.

For if you only looked for bad,
I knew that's all you'd see.
And that would make your life down here
So full of misery.

Now when my heart within me cries,
"Your death was so unfair!"
It's almost like I hear you say,
"You're right, Mom, life's not fair!"

"You need to start to look for good ~
If all you see if bad,
The rest of your life here on earth
Will always stay so sad."

It's just as if the words I said
Keep echoing at me.
Refusing from my mind to rest,
Until I finally see.

Life's not fair ~ I knew it then,
And even more so now.
But while I've life, I'll look for good
In everything---------somehow.

YOU'RE NEVER FAR AWAY

By Judy A. Andres
03/18/94

You're never very far away,

You're in my thoughts both night and day.

And though it fills my heart with pain,

My eyes still search for you in vain.

The memories within my heart,

Tear at it 'til it's torn apart.

The pieces falling down like rain,

Incessant, never-ending pain.

Mere words cannot begin to tell,

The pain I've grown to know so well.

There are no words to best express,

The shattered dreams ~ the loneliness.

And still, no matter how I try,

There's not a moment passes by,

That you're not very far away ~

In every thought of every day.

DEEP LONGING

By Judy A. Andres
03/19/94

I have a longing deep within
To have you back on earth again.
But that would be to you unfair,
For nothing here could e'er compare.
Heaven's all that's peace and love,
You're with the Father up above.
You now enjoy contentment rare,
For you are in the Master's care.

JUST AWAY

By Judy A. Andres
03/19/94

"She is not gone ~ she's just away."

I hear a voice within me say.

"Mourn no more because she's dead.

She will no more have aching head.

She'll cry no more. That all is passed.

Her heart that broke will mend at last.

All earth's trials for her are through.

A new day dawned ~ It's all brand new.

What's it like? I've not been there.

But God says we'll have no more cares.

I'll trust in Him. He is my friend.

And I'll be with them in the end.

It's now as though I hear her say,

"I am not gone, I'm just away!"

THE MIGHTY OAK

By Judy A. Andres
03/19/94

The mighty old oak tree stands there,

And even with its branches bare,

It offers rest to passers by –

The ones that travel in the sky.

They stop and rest there for a spell.

I wish their tales they'd share as well,

Of all they see with their bird eyes

Of us, who sit down here and cry.

For they have seen us come and go

For days now as our tears do flow.

I almost feel the tree and birds

Have become my best friends.

SIDENOTE: *There is a huge old oak tree in the cemetery near where Jenni is buried. I use to go sit there all the time, and I would gaze at it and watch the birds*

TIME GOES BY

By Judy A. Andres
03/19/94

Another moment passes by,
And soon an hour's through.
The hours pass on into days,
While I am missing you.

Those days have turned to weeks, then months,
And months have turned to years.
It seems as though 'twas yesterday ~
But I've shed so many tears.

Time can't turn back, nor be stayed,
For time continues on.
It stops not for anyone,
But trudges ever on.

The seasons pass, and time does too,
But this one thing is true.
As long as I have breath to live,
I'll still be missing you.

YOUR 21ST BIRTHDAY

By Judy A. Andres
04/11/94

It's another birthday, Jen ~

Your 21st it would have been.

But now we've only memories

Of "yesterdays" and "use to be's."

Your death our lives forever changed.

Our hopes and dreams have rearranged.

But times like this we still hold dear.

You may have died, but you're still near.

You're in our thoughts, and in our hearts,

And so we know you'll not depart.

Your birth we still can celebrate.

You touched our lives, that part was great!

TO PA

By Judy A. Andres
04/11/94

It's 2 years now since you were here ~
We still can see your face.
So many precious memories
That time just can't erase.
Your gardens and your rose bushes,
We always did admire.
You knew about so many things,
Amazing knowledge you'd acquired.
Deer hunting, wood cutting, and tractor rides,
Chicks, ducks, and guinea hens.
Bluebird houses you'd put up,
Building projects---porches and pens.
There were card games at the cottage,
Picking berries, feeding chipmunks
like a little boy.
You always made sure our kids were overstocked
With candy, snacks and toys.
Your sons, I know, are proud of you,
And so are all their wives.
And I know that I speak for all,
"We'll miss you all our lives."
BUT, the memories you've given us
Will last 'til the end of time.

EVEN THOUGH

By Judy A. Andres
06/27/94

Even though I know that you are
in a better place,
It doesn't change the fact I long
to see your precious face.
It doesn't change the longing that lies
unquenched deep within,
To hear your voice, to feel your touch,
to have you back again.
It doesn't end the loneliness
nor ease this pain I feel,
Even though you're in His care
this pain is oh, so real.
I feel as though a part of me
died on the very day
That Jesus came and called you home,
seemingly a tragic way.

With every day that passes

I yet die a little more.

The loneliness is killing me ~

and that I can't ignore.

So on the day my heart no longer

beats another beat,

And my soul from within me

takes its flight and doth retreat,

T'will not be from disease nor age,

but broken heart and grief,

That finally lays my pain to rest,

and brings such sweet relief.

UNANSWERED QUESTIONS

By Judy A. Andres
07/11/94

Unanswered questions
Still gnaw at me.
Wish I had answers
So they'd let me be.
It wouldn't change things,
Yes, I know that's true ~
But at least I would finally know
Just what happened to you.

A WORLD APART

By Judy A. Andres
07/11/94

It seems as though I'm living
In a world apart from here.
A spectator of life once lived,
Now looking in a mirror.

I see life go on around,
But it seems so unreal.
It's almost like I'm watching ~
But not allowed to feel.

PAIN

By Judy A. Andres
08/23/94

As I look about me,

Pain is all I see.

There is death and dying,

Throughout all humanity.

There are no exemptions,

No clauses or loopholes.

A respecter of persons ~ NOT!

Death claims young, as well as old.

SIREN SERENADE

By Judy A. Andres
08/23/94

There was a siren serenade,
On that October night.
I listened as I lay in bed ~
I knew something wasn't right.

I wondered as I listened,
To all their mournful sounds,
"What could possibly have happened
For them to all be called?"

The Sheriff with his siren on
Was rushing to the scene,
With ambulance and fire trucks ~
Oh no, what could that mean?

My heart began to sink inside,
I knew you were not home.
But it was early in the night ~
My thoughts began to roam.

I thought, "Something very tragic
Must have happened to someone.
I hope it's no one that I know" ~
And that's when our phone rung.

I tried to quiet all my fears
By thinking of times past.
I wished that time would quickly fly,
So you'd be home at last.

I didn't want to answer it,
Yet, what if it was you,
Wanting to say you'd be late,
Oh, then what would I do?

I hesitantly picked it up,
But the voice that was there,
Was not yours, and then I knew ~
My heart broke beyond repair.

The worst that could have happened, happened.
My nightmare had come true ~
I now would spend my life on earth
Forever without you.

I MISS YOU JEN!

FEELINGS

By Judy A. Andres
09/23/94

I feel as though You turned Your back
On all of us who prayed,
Asking You to spare her life ~
I feel almost betrayed!
I feel a turmoil deep within,
And wonder where You were.
I feel as though all hope has died ~
My future left with her.
I feel as though I'll lose my mind ~
As though You're far away.
It feels like such a waste of time,
And such a chore to pray.
But, though these are the things I feel,
I still know that You're real.
Oh, I'm so glad Your love does not
Depend on how I feel!

LONELINESS
AND
SADNEESS

By Judy A. Andres
01/17/95

Loneliness and sadness
Sometimes o'erwhelm my heart,
Creeping o'er my being ~
Tearing me apart.

But every day that passes
Brings me one step closer home.
All life's trials over ~
Eternal peace will be my own.

So help me, Lord, to trust you
When I do not understand.
Help me not to falter
When things go not as I'd planned.

EMPTINESS

By Judy A. Andres
01/24/95

Sometimes the emptiness inside
Consumes my every thought.
It makes even my waking hours
Seem useless, and for naught.
It robs me of much needed sleep,
When sleep is what I need,
To ease this pain and loneliness
So I can pay no heed.
No heed to all the endless hours
Of knowing you're not there.
And wondering just where God was,
Or does He even care?
No heed to all the others who
Still have their daughters here.
Enjoying all the things we planned
or all those future years.
The memories that come to mind,
Reminding me of you ~
If I had not those memories,
I wonder what I'd do.
The times we had, I'll treasure,
Until the day I die.
Yet here I still am questioning ~
Forever wondering, "Why?"

WHENEVER GOD FEELS FAR AWAY

By Judy A. Andres
01/24/95

Whenever God feels far away ~
Remember He is near.
Whenever you are sore afraid ~
Remember not to fear.
Whenever life seems oh so dark ~
Remember He's the Light.
And if you sink into despair ~
Remember that's not right.

CHORUS:
'Cause Jesus wants to be your friend,
He wants to be your guide.
A very present help in trouble, always by your side.
So right now if you ask Him in your heart,
He'll answer you.
And Jesus will be your friend, too.

Whenever no one's listening ~
Remember He still hears.
He knows things you've left unsaid,
and He knows all your fears.
Whenever you have lost your way ~
Remember He's your guide.
Whenever no one stands by you ~
Remember He's by your side.

CHORUS

So if your eyes should fill with tears ~
Remember His did too.
Whenever you feel so unloved ~
Remember He loves you.
And if you're feeling lost, alone ~
Remember He's the Way.
Whenever everyone has gone ~
Remember He will stay.

CHORUS

Now whenever you feel friendless ~
Remember He's your friend.
His promises are faithful,
and they will be to the end.
Jesus is the Truth, the Life,
He is the only Way.
So open up your heart to Him,
and He'll come in to stay.

CHORUS

SAD AND BLUE

By Judy A. Andres
01/26/95

When I am feeling sad and blue,
I only have to turn to You,
Remembering the things You do,
And then I'm not so sad.

For when I feel alone and lost,
I only have to count the cost,
Of all You did upon the cross,
Then things don't seem so bad.

When all earth's cares close in on me,
I only have to turn to Thee,
For only You can set me free,
From all that makes me sad.

When I at last reach Heaven's shore,
Free of earth's cares forevermore,
Again with those who've gone before,
Then I shall be so glad!

SOMETHING INSIDE ME

By Judy A. Andres
01/27/95

Something inside me still cries out in pain.
Something inside me still searches in vain.
Searches for answers that will never be.
Searches for reasons He took you from me.

Something inside me lies empty and cold.
Something inside me longs for you to hold.
It searches for answers that never will be.
And, too, for the reasons He took you from me.

Yet something inside me keeps memories alive.
That something inside me helps me to survive.
Survive without answers that never will be.
Survive without reasons He took you from me.

THE CROSS WE CARRY

By Judy A. Andres
01/27/95

What is the cross you carry

As you go from day to day?

What is the burden that you bear

Along life's rocky way?

What is the sorrow that you have ~

The one you're sure won't heal?

What is the pain that daily taunts ~

The one that is so real?

What causes all the loneliness

And sadness that you feel?

What hinders you from praying now

And asking God to heal?

For He's the Great Physician,

And He wants to heal your pain.

He wants to help you bear your load ~

Quit floundering in vain!

TRUTH TO PONDER

By Judy A. Andres
01/31/95

Why do I question

the things that He does,

when I know that He's out there,

and watching in love?

MY REFUGE

By Judy A. Andres
01/31/95

Precious Savior, You're my refuge

from the storms of life so bleak.

You alone can lift my spirit,

for You know I am too weak.

ILLIUSIVE BUTTERFLY

By Judy A. Andres
01/31/95

Like an illusive butterfly

Your memories flutter through

The flowery meadow of my mind,

And I am there with you.

A moment, but a fleeting glimpse

Of yesterdays we shared.

So real I seem to feel again

All of the love we shared.

So I reach out ~ embrace each one,

But every time I do,

They flutter off, and fade away,

And I'm left missing you.

IN MEMORY OF
JEN'S 22nd BIRTHDAY

May 29th

Written April 25, 1995

Your birthday comes around each year ~

It has been 4 since you were here.

Now only in my memory ~

I long for how it used to be.

Before we'd always celebrate ~

With joy we would anticipate.

But now each comes and goes with pain.

You cannot come, I wish in vain.

You cannot come to me, that's true,

But some sweet day I'll go to you!

PRECIOUS YEARS

By Judy A. Andres
04/27/95

In all the lonely days that pass,

I gaze as in a looking glass,

And see behind me, through my tears,

Those very precious 18 years.

The years that hurried by too fast,

And now that are forever past.

They have to last my lifetime through ~

Were an entire life for you!

UNFAIR!

By Judy A. Andres
04/27/95

So many things in life ----unfair.

We see them happen everywhere.

Just look around at all the pain.

It happens time and time again.

Day after day, night after night.

So many things that just aren't right.

An accident, a homicide.

Or even senseless suicides.

They claim the lives of those we love.

We look for answers from above.

There are no answers to us given.

No answers----none this side of Heaven.

And when at last we all get there,

I don't suppose we'll even care.

For when we see your face at last,

All of the pain will all be past.

22nd BIRTHDAY

By Judy A. Andres
05/17/95

It's your birthday once again,

And though you are not here,

The memories, each one of them,

I hold so very dear.

It's true, you've gone now from this earth,

But, Jen, year after year,

You're always close in mind and heart,

So, you're still very near.

BURDENED?

By Judy A. Andres
05/19/95

Are you ever burdened down with loads of care?

Are you ever helpless, or drowning in despair?

Are you ever weary and longing to be free...

Of this life here on earth

With all it's misery?

Turn to Jesus, He really cares!

Turn to Jesus, He hears your prayers!

Turn to Jesus, He'll see you through!

Turn to Jesus, He cares for you!

WONDERING WHY?

By Judy A. Andres
06/29/95

Do you ever wonder why

things happen as they do?

Why things come into our lives

that make us oh, so blue.

Sometimes it seems like everything

that happens turns out bad,

And we're left feeling so forlorn,

and very, very sad.

Yet other times, to our surprise,

when things seem at their worst,

There comes a ray of sunshine ~

Just one solitary burst.

Enough to give us what we need,

the strength to travel on

Along the rocky road of life,

until God calls us home.

ACHEY SOUL

By Judy A. Andres
07/12/95

There is an ache within my soul

A sadness that I can't control

In time t'will surely take its toll

And soon all eyes will see

That living life without you now

With memories that hurt somehow

For I must keep them hidden now

T'will be the death of me!

TEARS

By Judy A. Andres
08/19/95

My tears don't flow in public now,
So when they look at me,
They think that grief has finally passed,
And I must better be.

Because they see me smile and laugh,
They've mistakenly assumed
That it is going well with me,
And life I have resumed.

But they don't know, how could they see?
There's no way they could know,
The pain I live with every day,
I'm glad they'll never know.

Though I have learned to hide it well,
So well that most can't see,
The pain is still there every day,
I know t'will always be.

THREE YEARS, TEN MONTHS
TWO WEEKS

Time marches on...

By Judy A. Andres
08/20/95

Three years, ten months and two weeks now
Since I have seen your face.
It seems like such a long, long time
To go without embrace.

Yet yesterday I spoke with you ~
No, it's been years ago.
Compared to all eternity
That is not long, I know.

Still I keep wishing years would pass
As though they're only days.
T'would help to ease this loneliness ~
Suppose there's just no way.

No way to alter my time here,
Can't shorten it ~ What for?
For when I'm finally Home at last ~
Won't matter anymore!

ALONE

By Judy A. Andres
08/28/95

Each night as I sit alone
And watch a day go by,
I find myself just sitting here,
And still I wonder "Why?"

Why others go on living,
Who waste their lives away.
And you were taken while so young ~
Not given one more day.

There are those who do not care
For anyone but self.
And other who kill needlessly,
And those who kill themselves.

It just all seems so senseless!
I'll never understand!
No matter how I look at life,
I cannot know His plan.

I must trust my Lord knows best ~
He knows what's best for thee.
And some sweet day we'll meet again
For all eternity!

TIME CAN'T HEAL

By Judy A. Andres
08/28/95

Time cannot heal this pain I feel,

No, time is not my friend.

It only doth prolong the pain,

And taunt me without end.

For if Time were a friend of mine,

It surely would have ceased,

The day your life was ended,

And mine was filled with grief.

HERE I SIT...

By Judy A. Andres - 08/28/95

Here I sit, I'm sad and blue.

And yes, I am still missing you.

I'm feeling lonely once again.

Almost as though I have no friends.

It seems they've all abandoned me,

And left me in my misery.

I know they think that I have changed.

It's true, my life's been rearranged.

I act not as I did before,

Which makes them leery and unsure.

I guess, uncomfortable, at best ~

Which leaves them feeling deep unrest.

For when they look at me they see

Just how unhappy they could be

If suddenly their child was gone ~

How bad they'd feel, as if they're wronged.

I think the realization's there

And plain for them to see

That it could happen to them, too,

As it happened to me.

FADED TIME

By Judy A. Andres
08/28/95

I knew that time would fade away
Your memory from their minds.
I knew that they'd eventually
Pick up what they'd left behind.

I knew that as this happened
I would feel you'd been betrayed.
And yet, I know t'would not be fair
if deep in grief they stayed.

I knew their visits to your grave
Would wane, and soon grow few.
I knew that was how it would be,
And how you'd want them to.

But as I see it happen,
I find I'm saddened, too.
For all those things to me were signs
They've not forgotten you.

And yet I know down deep inside
All of your friends who cared,
Have in no way forgotten you ~
Nor all the times you shared.

REGRETS

To My Son, Dan

By Judy A. Andres
08/29/95

I try so hard to make things now
Like they used to be,
In hopes that it will ease your mind,
And more of you I'll see.

I know it has been hard on you,
As it has been on me.
For when death took someone we loved,
It changed our family.

I know you try hard to forget
The pain her death has brought.
And watching you throughout these years,
A lesson I've been taught.

There is no way we can reclaim
The years that we have lost.
And looking back upon them now,
I sit and count the cost.

Because I've been consumed with grief,
And let it rule my day,
I've seen you pull away from us ~
You have just stayed away.

In grieving for the loss of Jen,
It has pushed you away.
It's something that I will regret
Until my dying day.

TRUST AND OBEY

By Judy A. Andres
08/30/95

When life hath dealt its very worst,
And I am feeling almost cursed,
So sad my heart just wants to burst,
It's then I hear Him say…
Trust and Obey,
For there's no other way.

When sorrow seems too much to bear,
It's then I wonder if He cares,
Or even if He's really there,
But then I hear Him say…
Trust and Obey,
For there's no other way.

When grief doth take its toll on me,
Am I so blind I cannot see,
All that my Savior's done for me?
Again I hear Him say…
Trust and Obey,
For there's no other way.

When there's no way to understand,
No way to see what's in His plan,
It's then I need to take His hand,
Heed what He says to me….
Trust and Obey,
For there's no other way
To be happy in Jesus,
I must Trust and Obey.

I LOVE YOU MORE...

By Judy A. Andres
09/08/95

I love you more

With the pass of each new day.

Wish I could tell you,

But there is no way,

To put into words

How I feel deep inside.

T'would be futile to try it,

Or I would have tried.

So, I'll try to show you

With things that I do,

Hoping you'll see

Just how much I love you.

DEATH VALLEY

By Judy A. Andres
09/08/95

The Valley of the Shadow
Of Death is real to me....
I now can say that it is real,
As real as real can be.

Yet even as I walk there,
I know He's by my side.
An ever-present help to me...
My Friend, My Strength, my Guide!

HOLD ON? LET GO?

By Judy A. Andres
06/14/96

When to hold on to,
And when to let go.
No one can tell you,
You've just got to know.
No one can dictate
The time or the place.
It's something that
Ultimately each one must face.
It's never easy
When that time comes.
You might not be ready.
I never was.
But when that time happens
I'm sure you will see,
When you've released them
How happy you'll be.
Happy to see
The person they've become.
Grown to adulthood,
Still, your daughter, your son.

THE WHY OF IT

By Judy A. Andres
Birthday 1996

I wish I knew "the why of it."

I wish I knew "the how."

I know it wouldn't change one thing ~

But, it might help somehow...

To understand why you are gone,

And why I am left here.

How it could happen on that night,

To one I hold so dear.

As long as I am wishing

For things that cannot be...

I wish that you were safe and well

And back on earth with me.

IT WAS FOR ME

By Judy A. Andres
06/1896
(¾ Timing)

So many things here in my life,
I don't understand.
And yet I'm sure they're all a part
of my Master's plan.
When I get down, I need to look around and see...
All that He's done for me.

CHORUS:
It was for me God sent His Son to pay my penalty.
It was for me that Jesus bled
and died on Calvary.
It was for me He gave His life to set me free.
Praise God, Christ died for me.

I may not know why trials come into my life.
Why I feel lost, alone at times, so full of strife.
When I get down, I need to go to Him in prayer
Because He's shown me that He cares.

CHORUS
It was for me God sent His Son to pay my penalty.
It was for me that Jesus bled
and died on Calvary.
It was for me He gave His life to set me free.
Praise God, Christ died for me.

I cannot know just what tomorrow might bring.
I need not worry about anything.
My Savior cares, and knows what's best for me...
And this one thing I know.

CHORUS
It was for me God sent His Son to pay my penalty.
It was for me that Jesus bled
and died on Calvary.
It was for me He gave His life to set me free.
Praise God, Christ died for me.

GOOD-BYES

By Judy A. Andres
06/19/96

We said good-bye just like before
In a flippant sort of way.
For we both thought that it would be
Just like any other day.

You left, we hugged, a quick passing hug ~
A formality at best.
We did not know t'would be our last ~
There'd be no more requests.

You'd never say good-bye again,
Nor ask for hugs at the door.
Your presence that I'd always loved
Would be present here no more.

We take so much for granted,
Each time we say good-bye,
Expecting that again we'll meet
After the day's gone by.

Yet if we'd ever stop and think,
And ponder for awhile...
Each time we say it, the reality is,
It could be our last good-bye.

THOUGHTLESS GOOD-BYES

By Judy A. Andres
06/20/96

How often do we say good-bye
To the dear ones we treasure,
Expecting to see them again ~
Make memories at our leisure.

We take so much for granted.
We say, "We'll find a way
To take the time for those we love.
We'll have so many other days."

We figure that tomorrow
We'll take the time, my friend.
We figure that tomorrows
Will go on without end.

Sometimes tomorrow never comes,
Lest we regret delay ~
Why put off for tomorrow,
What can be done today?

WHAT IF TOMORROW NEVER COMES?

By Judy A. Andres
06/20/96

What if tomorrow never comes?
What if they leave today?
What are the things that you'll regret?
What things have you delayed?

What if you planned to take the time?
What if it was tomorrow?
What if all time for them runs out?
How great will be your sorrow?

What if no chance to say good-bye?
What if the end were now?
What are the things you've never said,
And put off 'till tomorrow?

We take so much for granted.
We say, "In time we'll find
The time for those we treasure most"...
BUT, Time's not always kind.

GET ON WITH IT

By Judy A. Andres
06/21/96

Get on with your life
I hear them say.
It's almost 5 years now
Since she went away.
That's plenty of time
To pick up your life.
So get on with it now.
Don't let it cause strife.
She may be gone now,
That part is true,
But you are still here,
So don't stay so blue.
Pick up the pieces,
Stop looking so sad.
If you really try hard
It won't be so bad.
But they've never been here.
There's no way they'd know.
If you're not here with me
I'd just as soon go.

JESUS

By Judy A. Andres
06/26/96

If Jesus were to come to earth

To spend the day with us,

I wonder if we'd have to change

The things done, or discussed.

I wonder if the things we think

Would even pass the test.

Or would the thoughts deep in our minds

Have to change with the rest?

It really shouldn't be that way ~

Our talk should match our walk.

And we should strive to be like Him

In every deed and thought.

IS IT ANY WONDER?

By Judy A. Andres
06/26/96

Is it any wonder that
I seem preoccupied?
And things I used to know before
Seem now from me to hide?
Why simple tasks seem complicated,
Drudgery, and a bore.
I can't begin to do the things
I did before.
"Before", ah yes, now there's the key
Unlocks this mystery!
The reason that my life's a mess
Is you're not here with me.

LIFE

By Judy A. Andres
09/30/96

Life's now very hard for me.

It's nothing like it used to be.

I wonder how I will survive,

With all this pain and hurt inside.

I wonder when the hurting's done,

If any vict'ries I'll have won.

Or if I will look back and say,

I've wasted each and every day.

FIVE YEARS

By Judy A. Andres
10/17/96

For five years now I've woke each day
and prayed for strength to meet
the empty, lonely feelings that
make living such a feat.

Though days roll by, and now years, too,
I still have come to find,
no matter how much time has passed
you never leave my mind.

You're with me every time I wake,
and yet when day is through,
I find that you're still on my mind...
Forever missing you!

MIRACLE OF BIRTH

By Judy A. Andres
03/24/97

A birth is such a miracle

An awesome act of God.

A day that we all celebrate

Each year, thereafter, on.

Yet when your day comes 'round each year

There's joy mingled with pain.

Today you'd have been twenty-four

If you'd survived that day.

But life gives us no guarantees,

Nor promise of long years.

We'll treasure all eighteen we had

And hold each very dear.

HAPPY 24th BIRTHDAY, JEN!
Love, Mom, Dad & Dan

MY THOUGHTS

March 26, 1997

Each day there is a turmoil that lies beneath the surface of my seemingly calm and serene composure. Feelings that I keep tucked away inside that are suspended in the emptiness that you left behind. They haunt every waking moment, and rest only in dreamless sleep...to wake again with each new daybreak. They are tireless, although they weary me, and sometimes wear my emotions thin. Emotions...a curious lot that I find mixed between wanting to remember, and trying to forget. How does one remember only what eases the agonizing grief that is a daily companion, and block out the memories that constantly inflict so much pain? How can constant reminders of your existence be so conflicting? I want to remember everything, yet in every memory there is the reality that you are no longer. You are a memory I want to remember, always. Your passing, a memory I long to forget.

MEMORIES

Judy A. Andres
09/25/97

Time can't erase the memories

Of those we hold most dear.

They deepen and endear themselves

As we pass from year to year.

SIX YEARS

Written by
Judy A. Andres
01/06/98

So often as I think of you

my eyes fill up with tears.

It doesn't seem to matter that

it's been all of six years.

Six seems like an eternity...

Sometimes like yesterday,

since your existence here on earth

ended tragically that day.

It really doesn't matter how...

Or even matter when...

The fact that you're no longer here

is torture without end.

ANOTHER DAY, ANOTHER YEAR

Written by
Judy A. Andres
01/06/98

Another year has started, Jen.

Another lonely year,

in which I'll only see your smile

in memories I hold dear.

The sound of your voice echoes deep

Within my hollowed heart.

The warmth of hugs and kisses that

you'll never more impart.

Each lingers on in memories

I cling to everyday,

and pray for strength to carry on ~

yet another day.

MY SELFISH WISH

Written by
Judy A. Andres
01/13/98

With angel wings your soul did mount

up heavenward that day.

And as the sun rose in the east

there were no words to say.

It must have been a glorious sight

there on the other side.

I'm sure our Savior welcomed you

with arms stretched open wide.

How peaceful to exist a place

where there is no more pain.

No fear, no discontentment,

nor striving, all in vain.

You are now with our Savior.

You're safe, I should not fear.

It's just that I'd give anything,

if you were safe back here.

SHADOWS IN MY MIND

Written by
Judy A. Andres
01/06/98

There's not a day that passes,
And not an hour goes by,
But that I wonder aimlessly,
Through shadows in my mind.

The shadows are the memories,
Of ones I love who've passed,
Away from this life here on earth,
To realms of splendor vast.

There's comfort in my knowing,
That though they're gone from view,
They have not left me totally,
From earth, they're gone, that's true.

Yet they are here beside me,
Their mem'ry helps me survive.
And spending time with them in thoughts,
Helps me keep them alive.

A TRIBUTE TO COMPASSIONATE FRIENDS

Written by Judy A. Andres ~ 1998

Compassionate Friends...
They mean so much to those who are bereaved.

Compassionate Friends...
They're always there, for us in time of need.

Compassionate Friends...
They lend their ears. They listen patiently.

Compassionate Friends...
They know our pain. They've been there,
don't you see.

Compassionate Friends...
They understand the pain we feel inside.

Compassionate Friends...
With them there is no reason we should hide.

Compassionate Friends...
Our every thought with them we're free to share.

Compassionate Friends...
Innermost thoughts... To them our souls we bare.

Compassionate Friends...
We never fear just how they'll react.

Compassionate Friends...
They're there for us as though we had a pact.

Compassionate Friends...
When others fail they never let us down.

Compassionate Friends...
True comfort just in knowing they're around.

Compassionate Friends...
For all these years it has been time well spent.

Compassionate Friends...
I truly feel they're surely Heaven sent.

Compassionate Friends...
We thank each one for giving of themselves.

DEEP SADNESS

Written by
Judy A. Andres
07/27/98

The close of the day brings a sadness,
Far different from that of the start.
An emptiness felt deep inside me.
Another day spent in my heart.

I gaze at immortalized memories,
The photos of times that were shared.
And long to go back into those days,
Times I thought t'would always be there.

But fate plays cruel tricks on us mortals.
It's so true, life's not always fair.
But that doesn't make it the easier,
To go on here while you're not there.

THINGS I TREASURE

Besides my family,
which goes without saying.

Written by
Judy A. Andres
07/27/98

The things I treasure most on earth

Cannot be bought or sold.

No value can be placed on them,

They're worth far more than gold.

Kind words, kind deeds, a friend, a smile,

A gentle, loving touch.

These are the things I cherish most...

The things that mean so much.

In Loving Memory
JENNIFER LYN ANDRES

05/29/73 to 10/06/91

How often the important things
Seem to go unsaid.
Like telling someone they are loved ~
Impossible when dead.

We take it all for granted,
At least we think they know,
How very much they mean to us,
But have we told them so?

For eighteen years were all we had~
Then death called you away.
And you were taken from us on
That cold October day.

Forever Missing You, Jen
Love Mom, Dad & Dan

TREASURED DAYS

Written by
Judy A. Andres
09/15/98

We must treasure every day,
Not wishing them to speed away.
For in a life there's way too few,
Regardless of the length.

Eighteen were all that you were giv'n
Before you were called up to Heav'n.
And looking back we need to say,
Thank God for the length.

Though some are granted so much more,
Some are given less.
So we must treasure those we had,
Remembering the best.

LOVINGLY REMEMBERING YOU
TODAY...AND ALWAYS, JEN.
Love, Mom, Dad & Dan

PIECES

Written by
Judy A. Andres
09/15/98

Pick up the broken pieces,
The shattered plans and dreams
That lay scattered about my life,
So burdensome they seem.

A heavy load to carry,
That once seemed oh so light,
Before your life was taken on
That cold October night.

How does one go about it?
How does one carry on,
When half everything they've lived for
So suddenly is gone?

GIVE IT ALL

Written by
Judy A. Andres
09/16/98

What are the words that best express

The emptiness...the loneliness

That haunts my every waking hour,

And saps life's energy and power,

Until I feel I can't go on?

It's then I hear Him say,

"I know your pain, I feel it, too.

That's why I'm always there for you,

To soothe your hurt, to ease your pain.

Why do you struggle on in vain?"

GIVE IT ALL...
GIVE IT ALL TO JESUS!

HERE TO STAY

Written by
Judy A. Andres
10/16/98

There is a never-ending pain

That aches within my heart.

It nags at every waking hour,

And tears me all apart.

This pain, it seemed to move right in

The day you went away.

As far as I can ascertain

It has moved in to stay.

IRREPARABLE DAMAGE

Written by
Judy A. Andres
10/16/98

I'll never really figure out

Why life continues on.

Within my chest my heart still beats,

While half of it is gone.

It seems a contradiction,

And yes, somehow unfair,

That mine can go on beating,

Damaged beyond repair.

WHAT, WHY & WHEN?

Written by
Judy A. Andres
10/16/98

What is this sadness that I feel?
Why won't it go away?
Why must I wake to find it there,
Each and every day?

Why does it intertwine itself
With everything I do?
Why can't I pick the pieces up?
Why did you tell me to?

Why can't I get control of it?
Why must it linger on?
Why does it so consume my life?
When will it be gone?

In Loving Memory
JENNIFER LYN ANDRES

05/29/73 to 10/06/91
October 1997

For six years your presence
Has been here with me ~
In pictures, in photos,
And in memories.
It cannot replace you,
It only consoles.
Jen, living without you
Has sure taken its toll.
But I am rejoicing
For one thing I know ~
There's coming a day
When we both will be Home!
Again reunited,
Together at last.
Forever together…
Our sorrow all past.

Love,
Mom
Dad &
Dan

In Loving Memory of
JENNIFER LYN ANDRES

05/29/73 to 10/06/91
26th Birthday – May 29, 1999

Jen, twenty-six you'd be today ~
If October '91 hadn't taken you away.

Eighteen years were all you got to see.

To me, eighteen you'll always be.

I'll cling to memories I was given,

'till we're reunited someday in Heaven.

In Loving Memory of
JENNIFER LYN ANDRES

05/29/73 to 10/06/91
October 1999

I do not need roses

To bring you to mind.

Nor do I need perfume,

You know the kind.

I never need places

That we used to go.

Nor memories of those times

Of so long ago.

For there's not a moment

In sunshine, or rain,

That you are not with me

What JOY....yet what PAIN.

Love,
Mom

In Loving Memory of
JENNIFER LYN ANDRES

05/29/73 to 10/06/91
28th Birthday
May 29, 2001

Birth ~ it's such an awesome gift,
Sent from God above.
For 18 years we had you here
To nurture and to love.

We have so many memories.
Your life was but a loan.
And God saw fit to take you home.
So now we celebrate alone.

In Loving Memory of
JENNIFER LYN ANDRES

05/29/73 to 10/06/91
May 29, 2002

Eleven birthdays come and gone,
since that October day.
Now memories of birthdays past
we celebrate today.

Love,
Mom

In Loving Memory of
JENNIFER LYN ANDRES

05/29/73 to 10/06/91
October 2002

Life goes on, I know that's true,
Now you are Aunt Jenni, too.
For Dan and Melissa had a son.
Benjamin Isaac, their first one.
But for him you'll exist only
In photographs and our memories.
And my heart will always ache...
FOREVER MISSING YOU.

Love,
Mom

In Loving Memory of
JENNIFER LYN ANDRES

05/29/73 to 10/06/91
In Celebration of Her
31st Birthday
May 29, 2004

There are no tears in Heaven,
God promises that's true.
But here on earth they fall like rain ~
Forever Missing You!

In Loving Memory of
JENNIFER LYN ANDRES

05/29/73 to 10/06/91
Written in September 2004

Though you've been gone for 13 years,
There's not a day goes by,
That you're not in my every thought,
And tears still fill my eyes.

A lot has happened in those years,
The ones that you've been gone.
You are an aunt again my love,
Lillian Jennifer Andres was born.
September 15, 2004.

Missing You Today, and Everyday ~
Forever Missing You!

WHAT MIGHT HAVE BEEN?

By Judy A. Andres
12/09/05

Jen, though you've be gone a long, long time,

The pain, it still remains.

You're in my thoughts still every day,

And time has not erased

My thoughts of what you might have done,

Or who you might have been,

With whom you might have spent your life,

Or how many grandkids I might have been given.

Whether you would live near, or far away,

I'll never know, and so I pray,

Lord, help me live my life down here

For those I love, who still are near.

And let me not waste another day,

Wondering what might have been.

I WONDER

By Judy A. Andres
12/30/05

Sometimes very late at night
When sleep won't come to me,
I sit and fantasize about
Just what you now might be.

I wonder if you'd live nearby,
Or very far away.
For out East was a favorite spot ~
Your friend lives there today.

Would you be off chasing dreams?
Or if a spouse you'd be.
Would your spouse be a gentle soul?
I sure would like to see.

I wonder what there'd be for kids ~
Children, light and fair?
Would they have your clear blue eyes,
And thick golden blonde hair?

Plans and dreams can change so fast ~
A moment, and they're gone.
And all that's left are memories of
Your life…an unfinished song.

MARRIAGE MADE IN HEAVEN

By Judy A. Andres
December 2005

A marriage made in heaven
Back so many years ago.
Now looking back with wonder ~
Where did all those years go?
Thirty-four have come and gone,
And things have taken place.
Some have been unbearable
While running our human race.
But you have stood beside me,
No matter come what may.
For when you said "I do", you did,
Back on our wedding day.
One thing that I have noticed
As the years have come and gone,
The more of time that passes,
Our love, it grows more strong.
The time I spend with you is dear,
And this one thing I know:
I'm thankful that I married you
So many years ago.

HOLIDAYS

By Judy A. Andres
12/21/05

Holidays have taken on
a different sort of hue.
The festive colors now just
do not seem to be so true.
The reds and greens are not as bright;
the tinsel's lost its luster.
To get into the mood at times
takes more than I can muster.
The carols do not sound the same,
but no one is to blame~
I long to see your smiling face,
hear someone call your name.
I have so much for which to praise
and give thanks to the Lord~
And seeing you again some day
is really a reward.
I need to spend my earthly time
making memories to treasure,
With Dad, Dan, Melly, Ben and Lily,
true treasures without measure.

CHRISTMAS IN HEAVEN

By Judy A. Andres
12/16/05

Christmas in Heaven...
What a glorious sight,
To be in a place where
Everything's right.

Christmas in Heaven...
What wonder affords
To be in that place ~
In the presence of our Lord.

Christmas in Heaven...
There's no finer place,
Than with the Lord Jesus ~
To see His dear face.

Christmas in Heaven...
With angels, Rejoice!
Sing praises to Jesus.
Lift up your voice.

Christmas in Heaven...
I long for that day.
With family and friends ~
Together always.

Christmas in Heaven...
What I wouldn't give,
To be where you are,
Rather than here where I live.

Christmas in Heaven...
You're lucky, you know.
I'll just keep on dreaming
Until I can go.

This is what my friend Ruth (Lytle) Bahr e-mailed me back:
Christmas in Heaven
My friend wants to go
How I'd live without her
I really don't know

Christmas in Heaven?
Isn't Christmas here too?
Isn't Christ with us,
In all that we do?

I know what you're saying
I know who you miss
But you have been given
A life full of bliss

A husband who loves you
To depths we can't tell
A Dan and a Melly
And grandkids as well

A home in God's country
Such beauty surrounds you
His breath softly whispers
His love all around you

Your life is so full
Your ministry strong
You must go the distance
No matter how long.

Christmas in Heaven
Must be glorious I know
But God wants us here
That Glory to show.

I love you,
rab

Photo of me and Ruth taken
in the summer of 2005.

A CHILD

By Judy A. Andres
12/31/05

A child is a gift from God,
A gift that we should treasure.
For there is nothing can compare
To this gift of love beyond all measure.

It doesn't matter what they do,
Matters not what they say.
They bring joy to our every breath
Throughout all of their days.

Bring them up to know His love,
Our heavenly Father up above,
Who gave His life that we might live.
Who by example taught to forgive.

So cherish God's gift from above,
And lavish them with all your love.
Not forgetting whence they came,
Praising your Father's holy name.

OUR GREAT TREASURE

Written by
Judy A. Andres
December 2005

Our children are treasures ~
A gift from above.
Someone to cherish,
To nurture and love.

More precious than silver ~
Or even than gold!
Of far greater value
than earthly wealth untold.

The years will go quickly…
Make memories that last.
Don't find yourself wishing
You could change the past.

For days will pass quickly,
The years will fly by.
They'll grow up so fast that
It may make you cry.

Please show them you love them ~
Don't just tell them it's true.
Train them up in the way
The Lord wants you to.

For they are a treasure ~
You'll see that it's true.
The only treasure from earth
You can take into eternity with you!

LONGING FOR HOME

By Judy A. Andres
03/13/06

There are times that I still feel
I wish my life would end.
Then I'd be home with you and Mom,
My grandparents and friends.

But God still has a plan for me,
Tis really very plain.
He gives me comfort day by day
To help to ease my pain.

For others here still need to hear
Of His great sacrifice.
To leave them dying in their sin
Would not be very nice.

So I will spend remaining days,
Sharing what I know.
'Til one sweet day He calls to me,
And I can homeward go.

MY FUNERAL POEM

To be read at my funeral,
when the time comes.

By Judy A. Andres

You've all gathered here today
Because I've gone away.
I'm in the arms of my dear Lord,
There I'll forever stay.

The Bread of Life, The Light, The Truth,
He is the only Way.
No one will come to where I am
Until they humbly pray.

Accepting all that Christ has done
Upon the cross that day.
He died, was buried, rose again ~
Now death can't have its way.

Though man is sinful right from birth,
And can't be free from sin,
The grip of sin is gone
When one is born again.

There is no other way to Heaven,
No works can man fulfill,
To earn a pass from here on earth ~
There's none will pay the bill.

Christ paid the debt He did not owe ~
Became the sacrifice.
All man need do is but believe,
For Christ has paid the price.

And so, rejoice, I am with Christ,
And those who've gone before.
Death has no sting, I'm happy now,
For I am with my Lord!

Those of you who know my Lord
I know I'll see again.
So until then, please live your life,
Exemplifying Him.

And share the Gospel message
With everyone you meet,
Until we walk together
On Heaven's golden streets.

Jen and I've been reunited.
Mom and Grandma welcomed me.
There will be no more parting.
Forever, together we'll be!

THE RETURN OF SPRING

By Judy A. Andres
03/14/06

I saw a robin Saturday...
a welcomed sign of spring.
And with it comes the promise of
new life for everything.

Leaves' buds will soon appear upon
trees' branches, bleak and bare...
and flowers, too, will poke up through
the earth, sparking a flare.

Soon color will return to view,
where now there's browns and grays.
Shades of greens, reds, yellows, pinks,
in quite a grand array.

The sky is such an azure blue.
The fluffy clouds, so white.
At times some showers from above,
with rainbows...what a delight.

The cold will turn to warmth again,
We'll shed those winter clothes.
We'll welcome all that spring will bring...
God's blessings overflow.

MORTAL WOUND

By Judy A. Andres
03/15/06

Just about the time I think

my life is in control,

I hear someone has shared my fate

And it tears at my soul.

It is as though the scab's been torn

Off from the deepest wound

That never does completely heal,

And salt's poured in the wound.

Then memories flood back to mind,

Ones I've tried to forget.

And each time that it happens

I know that's not happened yet.

My heart aches deep within me.

I feel again the pain they'll feel.

It is a mortal wound I've got,

And one that never heals.

SO FEW REGRETS

By Judy A. Andres
03/15/06

There is so much I'd like to say.
But I can't...you died that day.
And now I think of things unsaid,
Remaining so because you're dead.

So many things I long to change.
A second chance to rearrange
The hurtful things, not only words.
The things only you and I heard.

In this life it'd be quite nice
If before doing or saying we'd think twice.
There'd be less things we'd want to change,
And so few regrets.

HOMESICK FOR HEAVEN

By Judy A. Andres
03/15/06

I know this world is not my home,

I'm just a passing through.

And one day when my life here ends

I'll be at home with you.

I know that I can't go too soon

To my home in the air.

I'm sure that what I have down here

Will not even compare,

To all that He has promised those

Who put their faith in Him.

And one day soon I'll be with you,

And my Savior, and my friends.

HE CARRIES ME

By Judy A. Andres
03/15/06

This pain I live with every day
Would be the death of me,
If not for God's amazing grace ~
I know He cares for me.

He has not left me comfortless.
His promises are clear.
There's not a moment passes by
But that He's always near.

He is my refuge and my strength,
An ever-present guide.
He has promised He will stay
Always close by my side.

So when the days are darkest,
And I long for my death, too.
It's as if He whispers low,
My child, lean on my strength, I'll carry you.

I DON'T UNDERSTAND

By: Judy A. Andres
03/24/06

There are so many things in life
That make no sense to me.
I can't believe that this is right,
Or how its meant to be.

Why does God seemingly sit by
And watch my sorrows mount,
Trials and tragedies abound,
And then not help me out?

Sometimes I feel He's gone away
And left me here to wonder
If He even cares at all
When I stumble and go under.

But then I realize He knows,
He's been through every pain.
He's not a God that cannot feel ~
I bow my head in shame.

He cared enough to send His Son
To die for you and me.
His Son then suffered every pain,
So I should clearly see.

He has not left me comfortless
When I go through such pain.
And any suffering done on earth
Is really done in vain.

Unless I realize He's near,
And wants to comfort me.
He'll help me carry on down here
To share His Gospel, free.

There's others here who need to know
He cares so much you see.
And He still wants to use me,
So His witness I will be.

SHARED MEMORIES

Judy A. Andres
04/13/06

Whenever someone says your name,
Or a mem'ry shares,
I feel my burden lightened up,
As it shows me they care.

They know how much I long to hear
The music of your name.
For life without you here on earth
Just hasn't been the same.

They know I've mem'ries, too, of you,
And yet somehow they see,
It helps to ease the pain I feel
When they share theirs with me.

For when they share their mem'ries,
The ones that they hold dear,
My heart within me skips a beat,
And you still feel so near.

And even though you're gone away,
And no longer in view,
I cherish all the memories,
And I know they do, too.

THE VALLEY OF THE SHADOW OF DEATH

A mother's journey through the dark days of grief...
to a brighter tomorrow.

By Judy A. Andres

APPENDIX A

LIST OF THINGS TO DO

The following is a list of things I feel are helpful to know, when dealing with a person who has had a child die:

1. Be there. As hard as it may be for you to be around your family or friend who is grieving; be there!

2. Listen. You don't have to say a word. There really are no words that will help at a time like that. They need to talk, if they want, about their child, about what happened, or about whatever they want.

3. Talk. If they don't want to talk...just be there.

4. Cry. Don't be afraid to cry with that person. Tears are a healthy release...for the person, and for you.

5. Don't write, "Call me if there is anything I can do to help", because they will never call. They need you, but they won't call.

6. Don't use clichés such as, "It was God's will" and don't say, "At least you have other children." It doesn't matter how many children a person has. When one dies, it is devastating.

7. Please don't tell them what they "should" or "shouldn't" do. Each person will deal with things differently, and need to do so in their own way. For me, I needed photographs of Jenni still in plain view. Others may find that isn't right for them. But the key is that they have to do what is right "for them." No one can tell them what they need to be doing.

8. Be available. Don't just say you're available. Run errands for them, or help out in any way you see they could use help. It is so hard to even function doing daily routine things after a child dies. Any help you can offer is very helpful. Be specific about the task you are offering to do. Don't use generalizations.

9. Pay attention to any siblings that there may be. They are very hurt, too, and often ignored at a time like this. Never assume that they aren't hurting because they don't know how to express what they are feeling. Not only have they lost a sibling, their parents seem to be gone as well for quite some time.

10. Don't be afraid to say the deceased child's name. It does not cause pain to hear someone say their name. By saying the child's name it lets the parents know you haven't forgotten their child.

11. Share memories you have of the deceased child with the parents. Remember that there is never a moment when the child is not thought of, so don't figure because you don't mention them, it is far from the parents' mind.

12. Remember the family on important days, such as the child's birthday or death date, and send a card or note to the family, letting them know that you remember, too.

13. Never forget that recovery from grief takes time. Different amounts for different people. There is no set timetable for recovery from grief when a child dies.

14. Stay in contact with your friend or family member. Grieving does not end at the funeral. There are always a lot of people around for the funeral, but the days, weeks, and years afterward continue to be hard.

A very good organization that helps many parents who are grieving the death of their child is The Compassionate Friends. I attended a chapter in Madison, WI, after Jenni died, when the one in Portage ended. The following is contact information for anyone interested:

THE COMPASSIONATE FRIENDS
P.O. Box 3696
Oak Brook, IL 60522-3696
Toll Free: 877-969-0010

www.compassionatefriends.org

Madison Chapter:

Regional Coordinator/Directors:
Jim & Sharon Staniforth
4705 Eisenhower St.
Oregon, WI 53575
608-835-7493
Jimstan@charter.net

Outreach Coordinator:
Duane & Darlene Woldt
1202 Ellen Ave.
Madison, WI 53716
608-222-2125

Dwoldt@charter.net

Words that I modified to fit Jenni from the song that Cindi
Umstadt wrote for her mother-in-law's funeral:

SEE HER AGAIN

VERSE 1:

That October day, death had its way,
and Jenni was gone.
The sadness we feel in our hearts will not heal,
But our hope in Christ is real.

CHORUS:

Jesus, the promise that death
has lost its sting.
Jesus, by grace through faith in Him,
We will see her again.

VERSE 2:

Her light shone so bright as daughter and sister,
Granddaughter and friend.
The love she did sow in our hearts still grows,
But in this life its hard to let go.

VERSE 3:

Then one day, Christ will say,
"Come home" to us who remain.
There we'll gather on God's crystal shore,
And together we'll be once more.

ENDING AFTER THIRD CHORUS:

What a wonderful day that will be....
When we see her a-gain, when we see her a-gain!

PHOTO OF MY MOM

Gertrude B. Chapman
12/01/28 to 05/04/59

The following poetry my mom wrote before she died on
May 4, 1959. She had my grandmother give it to me,
along with the letter that she had also written to me on
January 22, 1959.

I ONLY KNOW

By Gertrude B. Chapman

I know not why my Jesus chose
A simple, humble life.
Nor walked the paths of this grim earth
With all its sin and strife.

I only know He walks with me,
This Savior so divine;
His gracious blessings to bestow
Upon such a wretch as I.

I only know He loved enough
To die on Calvary's tree.
And shed His precious blood
That I might be set free.

From bonds of sin which held me
Since the fall in Adam's time.
Praise God, I know He's Savior,
And I'm His and He is mine.

Written by:
Mommy
John 3:16

FULL SURRENDER

By Gertrude B. Chapman

My Jesus, how I love Thee.
I give myself to Thee.
As humbly now I do proclaim
Thy servant I will be.

I yield myself completely now
Before thy Great White Throne.
Take all my life and mold it
In accordance with Thine own.

Keep me humble, gentle Master
As with faith and trust in Thee;
I walk this earth of sin and strife
As Thou once did'st for me.

Make my feet to only go
On paths where Thou would'st trod.
Make my hands to labor for
The glory of my God.

Make my mouth to only speak
What's pleasing unto Thee.
Oh, Gentle Master, take me now,
Thy servant I will be.

So when I stand before Thy Throne,
On that Great Judgment Day.
"Come unto Me" will be the words,
I'll hear Thee Master say.

Written by:
Mommy
Matthew 6:24

A-8

TAKE UP THY CROSS

By Gertrude B. Chapman

"Take up thy cross and follow me,"
I heard the Master say.
"It was for you I bore the load
Of Calvary's Cross that day."

"Can you not bear awhile with Me
This cross of pain and strife;
When my grace is all sufficient
For your every need in life?"

"Take up thy cross and follow Me,
As on through life you trod.
Forever hovering over you
Is the loving hand of God."

"Take up thy cross and follow Me,"
Again I heard Him plead.
"For time will pass---release will come,
In Eternity, with Me."

Where pain and sorrow reign no more.
And Satan has no more way.
"Take up thy cross and follow Me,"
I heard my Master say.

Written by:
Your Mommy
Luke 14:27

SOMEONE CARES

By Gertrude B. Chapman

Someone cares and knoweth
What our needs be for each day.
We only need to yield our all
Trusting Him to lead the way.

When our hearts are heavy laden,
And the way, it seems so dim.
It's not that God's forsaken us.
But we, who have failed Him.

Though we don't always understand
Why sorrows flood our soul;
Away above the starry skies
Someone cares and knows.

Yes, Someone cares and knoweth
What our needs be for each day.
And His grace is all sufficient,
For each need---if we but pray.

ASK HIM!

Written by:
Your Mommy
I Peter 5:7

MOM'S LETTER

This is the letter my mom wrote to me before she died in May 1959:

January 22, 1959

My darling daughter Judy,

Even as I sit here writing this letter to you my darling, I realize that at its longest, our time together upon this earth will be short. It is because of this known fact, that I leave this letter as a source of comfort to you, should God call me home while you are yet so young.

Darling, things such as these do happen, we neither know nor understand why, no matter what age we are. It is one of the mysteries in life of which God alone is the author.

Though I (may) have been taken from you, Judy, you need never go on through life alone. This very God awaits your coming too someday. One day when He calls and the trumpet sounds I will search the streets of heaven for you, trusting my search will not be in vain. And as your mother, I'm sure it won't be, for your love for Jesus already gives to me much joy and memories such as these even death cannot destroy.

One thing I'd have you do my darling is continue on for Him, for you'll find no real lasting peace outside of His blessed fold. The dens of sin the world holds dear are not for us who love Jesus. Use the training your ever loving daddy and I have given you to serve Jesus. The gains of this world pass away, but what you store in eternal rewards never perishes.

I love you my darling, far exceeding any words I can ever write on paper. Though our bond of earthly love was great, a far greater bond of love is yours – that of Gods.

Claim your inheritance, for His love far excels any I have, or ever could offer. God's love is so superior that He gave Jesus for you that we may one day be reunited and never have to suffer parting again.

Jesus is the only way. Accept Him!

Be the kind of girl I've wanted you to be, but above all, be what God wants you to be. The cost is little compared to the price a suffering lost soul pays. God bless you, my darling, Judy.

Love,
Your Loving Mommy

A little over three months after mom wrote this letter to me, she died on May 4, 1959, after a long battle with breast cancer.

GRADUATION 1991
CHAPMAN FAMILY PHOTO

This is the photo that was taken at Jenni's graduation in 1991, since the whole Chapman family was together.

Front Row: Daniel Andres, Sara Sundsmo, Stephanie Sundsmo, Nathan Sundsmo
Middle Row: Jennifer Andres, Sonya (Chapman) Schultz, Mary Martin, Arden Chapman, Vivian (Martin) Chapman, Joanne (Chapman) Sundsmo, Jessica Sundsmo
Back Row: Judy Andres, John Andres, Mike Schultz, Amy Chapman, Stephen Chapman, Ronda Chapman, Philip Chapman, Rebecca Chapman, Russ Sundsmo, Carri Sundsmo

The photo was taken at Nelson Photography in Richland Center, WI.
Jim Nelson graciously allowed me to use this
and several other photos, in my book.

A-13

GRADUATION GROUP PHOTO
1991

Photo of Jenni with her two best friends at the graduation
ceremony in Richland Center, WI

Jacki Lingel, Jenni Andres, Jennifer Husnik

THANK YOU CARD

The thank you card that Jenni gave to her dad and I after she graduated in 1991, had the following hand-written note inside it:

Dear Mom & Dad,

I want you to know that I loved my graduation, and that if it wasn't for you guys, I don't know what I'd do. Graduation certainly wouldn't have been as special.

I have really appreciated everything you guys did in the past 18 years to prepare me for this time in my life. I know it must not be easy to be my parents...its not easy being me all the time either, but, if I didn't have the two of you behind me all the way, everything would be a lot more difficult.

I've made some pretty big decisions in the last year, with school and my life – and I've got a lot more to come. It scares me, but I feel a lot better knowing I'll have you guys to bounce my ideas off of.

My party was a lot of fun. Mom, it was perfect – Dad, my music wouldn't have hurt anyone a few decibels louder, but I understand. All in all – what's left to say but...

YOU'VE SPOILED ME!

Thanks a million.

Love, Jen

PHOTO OF BEST FRIENDS

It was a common practice at the time Jenni graduated to
have a "buddy picture" taken when you had your
graduation picture taken. Jenni had hers taken with
Jacki Lingel, her first friend after we moved
to Richland Center, WI.

Photo taken by Nelson Photography
of Richland Center, WI

(After she died, Jim Nelson graciously gave me all the negatives to the
photos he had taken of Jenni.)

PHOTO OF DAN & JEN

This photo was taken
at the airport
in Madison, WI,
as Dan was waiting to depart
for Hawaii the summer of 1991.

Jenni was going to be leaving
on her train trip
to New York later that month
with Jennifer Husnik.
She had said, "Quick, Mom, take a picture
of Dan and me getting along,
in case something happens
to one of us this summer."

PHOTO OF JENNI & JENNIFER
NEW YORK TRIP

Photo of Jennifer Husnik and Jenni leaving
from the train depot for the New York trip
during the summer after graduation
from Richland Center High School in 1991.

Jennifer Husnik and Jennifer Andres

NEW YORK

This is a photo that was taken while Jenni and Jennifer were in New York. The young man in the picture is Benjamin Vincent. While they were in New York, part of the time they stayed in a cottage that someone in Ben's family owned. He also was their guide while they were in upstate New York where he lives.

Jennifer Husnik, Jennifer Andres
& Benjamin Vincent

PHOTO OF JENNI
AND JENNY KRUEGER

This is a picture of Jenni and Jenny (Krueger) LaBatt that was taken from video that Jenni had done in the month or so prior to her death. My sister, Sonya Schultz graciously took the video and got some still shots off it for me, as I had no photographs of Jenni with Jenny. Jenny is the young lady that went to Madison with Jenni and Kevin the night of the accident. Jenny and her friend had driven separately so they could talk and get caught up on things. Her friend had just gotten out of the Marines.

This photo is taken off the video that Jenni had been doing the month before the accident. They were singing along to a song, with Jenni holding my teddy bear and Jenny holding the one I had bought for Jenni.

THE ANDRES FAMILY PHOTO - 1995

This photo was taken when Dan had his graduation photos done in 1994. Obviously, Jenni had been dead since October 1991, but I wanted her in the photo. I had the photographer have her graduation photo vignetted into our family photo. I asked him to put her graduation photo in an oval shape, with the edges faded around the oval, to indicate that she is still part of our family, even though she is gone. He misunderstood what I wanted, and at first had it look as though she were standing there with us. I initially had some explaining to do when the sample came for approval.

Photo taken by Nelson Photography of Richland Center, WI

FAMILY PHOTO OF DAN'S FAMILY
DAN, MELISSA, BENJI & LILY

This is a family picture of our son, Dan, and his wife, Melissa, their son Benjamin Isaac and daughter Lillian Jennifer taken April 2006. They are truly sunshine in my life. They have been there and helped me to my brighter tomorrows.

ROMAN BUNDY

My Little Brother
Big Brothers/Big Sisters Program

This photo of Roman and me was taken on a trip to a Brewer game in Milwaukee, with the Big Brother/Big Sister group from our area. It is just one of the many times we have enjoyed together. We are both avid movie goers, and he knows I won't take him to see anything that I wouldn't go to myself...which leaves out all non-family friendly movies.

PUPPIES
CHEYENNE

02/21/03 to 08/22/03

This is a picture of my puppy, Cheyenne, which was taken in July 2003 (she was killed in August 2003). Because of her death, being right there when it happened, and not being able to prevent it, staying by her side on the way to the vet clinic, standing next to her holding her while the vet examined her, talking to her the whole time, and she still died...I realized that I had to let go of not having been allowed to stay by Jenni the whole time she was dying. God used the death of my puppy to teach me this valuable lesson.

SHILOH

Born August 27, 2003
5 days after Cheyenne was killed.

We had bought Cheyenne from Ed & Trish Pillow near LaValle, WI. The day Cheyenne died, I had John call Ed and let him know what happened, and how sorry I was. I needed to know that Ed would let me get another puppy from him, because I had been very careful...it was just a horrible accident. Ed assured John that it would not be a problem, and he told us that new puppies were due any day, and once they were born we could go down and pick out the one we wanted.

We went down several times after the new puppies were born (from the same parent dogs as Cheyenne had been). When we had gotten Cheyenne, John had told me I could get one if there was a female left, and Cheyenne was the only female in that liter of four puppies. Therefore, there really was no choice involved. She was my only choice. However, when Shiloh was born, she was one of three...and they were all female puppies this time.

Ed didn't allow anyone else to choose a puppy until I made my choice. The day we went down to choose, I sat down on the floor by the puppies. Two ran away and hid, and Shiloh came running over to me and started playing with my fingers. She, herself, made the choice. She had the angel kiss I spoke of, the white spot on the back of her head. Shiloh, however, had two, about an inch apart. My daughter-in-law said that was because Jenni had kissed her, and Cheyenne had, too. We all smiled at the thought.

Shiloh's face is a mirror image of Cheyenne's. Although they do have the same parents, their dispositions are quite different. I suppose it is a lot like children in the same family. Each one has similarities, but they are unique in many ways.

When we went to leave with Shiloh, Ed wouldn't let us pay him for her. He gave her to us. What an amazingly kind-hearted gesture that was on his part.

PHOTO OF KEVIN & JENNI

This is a photo of Kevin and Jenni, taken on the weekend before their accident when Kevin went up to our relatives for Pa's last birthday party in September of 1991. I remember rushing to the store to get the film developed because I knew I had a recent picture of Jenni and Kevin from that previous weekend.

*Photo taken by Nelson Photography
of Richland Center, WI.
(After she died, Jim Nelson graciously gave me all the negatives
to the photos he had taken of Jenni.)*

JENNIFER LYN ANDRES
05/29/73 - 10/06/91

Gone Home, But Not Forgotten!

CONTRIBUTION INFORMATION

Anyone interested in making a contribution to the scholarship fund that was set up in memory of Jenni, can send their contribution to the following address:

UW Richland Campus
1200 Highway 14 West
Richland Center, WI 53581

Make the check payable to the Jennifer Lyn Andres Memorial Scholarship Fund.

Or, in the alternative, a contribution could be made in memory of Jenni by sending a check payable to The Compassionate Friends at the following address:

The Compassionate Friends
Pat O'Neal, Treasurer
4537 Pawnee Pass
Madison, WI 53711

Enclose a note with your check stating that it is being given in memory of Jennifer Lyn Andres.

The Compassionate Friends' mission is to assist families toward the positive resolution of grief following the death of a child of any age, and to provide information to help others be supportive. The Madison Chapter was founded in 1982.

Made in the USA
Middletown, DE
29 July 2022